SLEEP
ISSUES

Jay Vaughan and Alan Burnell
with Mary Wood, and Jayne Lilley

Published by
CoramBAAF Adoption and Fostering Academy
41 Brunswick Square
London WC1N 1AZ
www.corambaaf.org.uk

Coram Academy Limited, registered as a company limited by
guarantee in England and Wales number 9697712, part of the
Coram group, charity number 312278

British Library Cataloguing in Publication Data
A catalogue record for this book is available from the British Library

ISBN 978 1 910039 99 1

Project management by Jo Francis, Publications Department,
CoramBAAF
Photograph on cover from www.istockphoto.com
Designed and typeset by Fravashi Aga
Printed in Great Britain by the Lavenham Press
Trade distribution by Turnaround Publisher Services, Unit 3,
Olympia Trading Estate, Coburg Road, London N22 6TZ

For the latest news on CoramBAAF titles and special offers, sign up
to our free publications bulletin at https://corambaaf.org.uk/subscribe.

Contents

Notes about the authors

Alan Burnell is a registered social worker who qualified at Goldsmith's College London and progressed to an Advanced Diploma in working with children and families. He has been a local authority social worker and team manager of a fostering and adoption service. He left to become one of the initial counselling team at the Post Adoption Centre in London, where he eventually became director. In 1998, Alan was one of the founding members of Family Futures and for 20 years, until his retirement in 2019, he was Registered Manager of the agency.

Alan helped to pioneer post-adoption services for children and their adoptive families and has been at the forefront of integrating neuro-scientific research and theory into family placement practice in the UK. In 2015, he received a lifetime achievement award for his work in adoption.

Alan has contributed to many articles and books. He has also been involved in training parents and professionals involved in adoption, fostering and kinship care.

Jay Vaughan MA is a State Registered Dramatherapist, a Certified Dyadic Developmental Psychotherapist (DDP), a Theraplay Therapist and trainer, as well as a Somatic Experience Practitioner. Jay is Registered Manager and CEO of Family Futures, a voluntary adoption agency based in London. Jay has contributed to many articles and books and continues to consult and train around the UK on behalf of Family Futures, and still carries out some direct work with families and children.

Family Futures, founded in 1989, specialises in the assessment and treatment of traumatised children placed in foster families, adoptive families, special guardianship families or in kinship care. Family Futures offers an assessment and treatment programme called Neuro-Physiological Psychotherapy, which integrates Somatic Experience, Theraplay and DDP as part of the assessment and treatment approach.

Michael and Mary Wood have two active and loving sons. Their birth son, Oliver, is seven and excels at go-karting and maths. He always wanted a brother or sister. Their adopted son, Luke, is nearly two and joined the family when he was 11 months old. Luke was born with drug withdrawal symptoms and an inherited medical condition. In spite of this, he is strong and lovely to have around.

Jayne Lilley was born in the Midlands in 1972. She spends her life being Mum to two children, one by birth and one by adoption, being wife to Dan, and working in a finance department. In her spare time, she meditates, enjoys Spanish red wine and Italian food. She is the author of *Our Adoption Journey*, published by CoramBAAF in 2016.

The series editor
Hedi Argent is an established author and editor. Her books cover a wide range of placement topics. She has written several guides and story books for young children,

Acknowledgements
Thank you to all the team at Family Futures, as we would not have learned all we have learned without them. A special thank you to all the families we have worked with over the years from whom we have also learned so much.

Thank you particularly to Family Futures Assistant Psychologist, Dixie Noruschat, for her literature review, and to Mandy Ruddock, Sensory Integration Therapist, for her sensory integration information and strategies.

We are grateful to Dan Hughes, Ellie Johnson, Sarah Borthwick and Jennifer Ginger for reading and commenting on drafts of this book.

Looking behind the label...

Jack has mild learning difficulties and displays some characteristics of ADHD and it is uncertain whether this will increase...

Beth and Mary both have a diagnosis of global developmental delay...

Abigail's birth mother has a history of substance abuse. There is no clear evidence that Abigail was prenatally exposed to drugs but her new family will have to accept developmental uncertainty...

Jade has some literacy and numeracy difficulties, but has made some improvement with the support of a learning mentor...

Prospective adopters and carers are often faced with the prospect of having to decide whether they can care for a child with a health need or condition they know little about and have no direct experience of. No easy task...

Will Jack's learning difficulties become more severe?
Will Beth and Mary be able to catch up?
When will it be clear whether or not Abigail has been affected by parental substance misuse?
And will Jade need a learning mentor throughout her school life?

It can be difficult to know where to turn for reliable information. What lies behind the diagnoses and "labels" that many looked after children bring with them? And what will it be like to live with them? How will they benefit from family life?

Parenting Matters is a unique series, "inspired" by the terms used – and the need to "decode" them – in profiles of children needing new permanent families. Each title provides expert knowledge about a particular condition, coupled with facts, figures and guidance presented in a straightforward and accessible style. Each book also describes what it is like to parent an affected child, with either case studies or adopters and foster carers "telling it like it is", sharing their parenting experiences, and offering useful advice. This combination of expert information and first-hand experiences will help readers to gain understanding, and to make informed decisions.

Titles in the series deal with a wide range of health conditions and steer readers to where they can find more information. They offer a sound introduction to the topic under consideration and provide a glimpse of what it would be like to live with an affected child. Most importantly, this series looks behind the label and gives families the confidence to look more closely at a child whom they otherwise might have passed by.

Keep up with all our new books as they are published by signing up to our free publications bulletin at: https://corambaaf.org.uk/subscribe.

Titles in this series include:

- *Parenting a Child with Attention Deficit Hyperactivity Disorder*
- *Parenting a Child with Dyslexia*
- *Parenting a Child with Mental Health Issues*
- *Parenting a Child affected by Parental Substance Misuse*
- *Parenting a Child with Emotional and Behavioural Difficulties*
- *Parenting a Child with Autism Spectrum Disorder*
- *Parenting a Child with Developmental Delay*
- *Parenting a Child with, or at risk of, Genetic Disorders*
- *Parenting a Child affected by Domestic Violence*
- *Parenting a Child affected by Sexual Abuse*
- *Parenting a Child who has experienced Trauma*
- *Parenting a Child with Toileting Issues*

Introduction

Why is sleep important for healthy functioning?

If you ask any parent of a new infant what they struggled with most in the early days, weeks and months, it is probably sleep: how to get their new baby into a good sleep pattern and have sufficient sleep themselves. Struggling with sleep with a new baby is normal. And yet when we place children in new families, sleep is not usually discussed as an issue high on the agenda. However, it is essential to create good sleep patterns in order for the child to grow and develop into a healthy adult. There are four pillars of parenting infants and young children:

- sleep;
- food;
- toileting; and
- attachment.

Sleep is therefore of great importance to parents and children, and is a key indicator of health, not to be underestimated in its significance. If children are not sleeping well, then it is almost impossible for the other three pillars of parenting to be solid.

Sleep difficulties can be extremely challenging for the child as well as for the parent or carer, and can lead to conflict and distress. If sleep is not resolved, then as the problem progresses, the lack of sleep for both parties means that neither will be at their best for dealing with the difficulties.

Approximately 25 per cent of all children experience some type of sleep problem at some point during childhood but, of course, sleep problems are more prevalent in children and adolescents when there are underlying chronic medical, neurodevelopmental, or psychiatric conditions (Owens, 2008). This has been reflected in our clinical practice over the last 30 years. We are writing during the time of the Covid-19 pandemic and evidence is emerging that uncertainty and disrupted routines are having a detrimental effect on children's sleep patterns. It is not surprising then, that the majority of children who have come into the care system because of neglect and abuse, as well as infants who have been subjected to losses and transitions, have some degree of difficulty with sleep. Children may arrive in their prospective permanent families with the clear message that they slept fine in foster care, and yet when they move to their new family, they find it hard to sleep, to everyone's surprise, Other children, who were reportedly problematic sleepers in foster care, settle quickly in their adoptive family. It is hard to untangle this shift from foster to permanent family. Perhaps what is clear, and should be a given, is that moving a child from one family to another is inevitably going to bring to the fore issues that children are only able to easily express through sleep, food, toileting issues, and of course, challenging behaviour, but often distress is initially enacted through sleep. It makes perfect sense that a child on arrival in a new family should suddenly have extremely unsettled sleeping patterns. And one must not confuse adaptation with developmental progression. Many children who are, or have been, in care adapt, but at the cost of a more natural developmental progression.

CASE STUDIES

Joe (five years old), when placed with his adoptive parents, began to wake hourly during the night, screaming out for them and sobbing uncontrollably when they tried to comfort him. Joe had been fine and slept well in foster care but now was distraught. His adoptive parents were at a loss as to what to do, were increasingly exhausted and felt that this was not sustainable. With help and advice, they were able to put this behaviour into the context of their child's early history. One of our mantras is that parents and children need to go back before they can go forward, and we will be exploring what this means later in the book.

Tiger (three years old), when placed with her special guardians, slept throughout the night. She collapsed exhausted at 6pm, not waking until 7am or even 8am the following day. The carers were delighted at first that their fears about sleepless nights were unfounded. And yet Tiger was exhausted and seemed to be dragging herself through the day, unable to concentrate and spending the afternoon slumped on the sofa. With help, the carers came to realise that Tiger was actually not sleeping; she was in an extreme dissociative state at night and was not able to enjoy getting to know them or to settle into her new family during the day. In this instance, the carers were supported to find ways of gradually helping Tiger to relate to them, rather than being self-reliant and not allowing them to care for her. In time, Tiger was slowly able to develop a healthy sleep routine, that enabled her to drift off to sleep rather than to "opt out". This helped her to form a closer relationship incrementally with her special guardians.

It is important to emphasise that there are no simple solutions or quick fixes for problems relating to sleep, food, toileting, or attachment issues. Trauma in infancy and early childhood has a profound effect on subsequent child development. So, unless adoptive parents and foster carers are offered a more in-depth understanding of child development, you will find yourself attempting, as we have so often seen with many parents and carers over the years, to "push a cart uphill".

The next chapter will look at good sleep hygiene and the impact that trauma has on sleep. Our second and third chapters will be solution-focused. Section Two of this book includes comments on different approaches described by two families struggling with their children's sleep difficulties.

Note: Some of the terms used in this guide may be unfamiliar to readers. A glossary at the end of the book provides clear explanations.

UNDERSTANDING SLEEP ISSUES

JAY VAUGHAN AND ALAN BURNELL

CHAPTER 1

Good sleep hygiene and the impact of trauma on sleep

Sleep for children who are fostered or adopted is the focus of this book, because it is one of the key pillars for healthy child development. Sleep is the way in which we restore ourselves from the exertions and experiences of the day – not just our brain but our whole body requires it. We need to sleep in order to facilitate our neuro-physiological development, and sleep deprivation has a profound impact on the whole of our well-being, our ability to manage day-to-day life stresses, relationships and problem solving.

Sleep is not just a time of rest when we are unconscious, but an active process that helps us not only rest and recover, but also make sense of our world. During the course of the day, all of us accumulate a vast amount of information and experiences that need to be processed and sorted or discarded. This processing happens when we are asleep. Processing and storing information is how we, and in particular children, learn and acquire language, social and motor skills. As children's rate of growth is far faster than that of adults, they naturally require more sleep. Whilst adults require 7–9 hours of sleep a night, a one-year-old child needs 11–14 hours of sleep, and a school-aged child 9–11 hours of sleep. Children whose sleep patterns have been disrupted, or never established, will inevitably struggle to have the quality and length of sleep that they require.

What is a good sleep pattern?

There are three stages of sleep:

- **Stage 1** is the changeover from wakefulness to sleep.

- **Stage 2** is a period of light sleep before you enter deeper sleep.

- **Stage 3** is the period of deep sleep that you need to feel refreshed in the morning.

Within these stages, there are different kinds of sleep:

- **Rapid eye movement (REM) sleep** is a unique phase distinguishable by rapid movement of the eyes, accompanied by low muscle tone throughout the body, and the propensity to dream vividly.

- **Deep sleep**, unlike REM sleep, is when your body and brain waves slow down. It is hard to wake from deep sleep, and if you do, you may feel quite groggy.

- **Light or shallow sleep** is easier to wake from. External stimuli such as noise, temperature, touch, and movement can wake you. You will wake up more readily, with less effort, from light sleep than from deep sleep.

4

It is important for children (and adults) to have a long enough period of unbroken sleep in order to enjoy the benefits of each stage and variation of the sleep cycle.

Early infant sleep patterns are quite different from those of adults. Infants younger than six months spend 50 per cent of their sleep time in active rapid eye movement (REM) sleep compared with 20 per cent in adults. Infants enter sleep through an initial active REM stage, in contrast to adults, who do not enter REM sleep until about 90 minutes into their sleep cycle. Active REM sleep occurs more often in infant sleep cycles, which results in shorter cycles.

However, after the age of six months, the infant should begin to develop a more mature sleep pattern. After an initial "settling" period of 10–20 minutes, the infant should drift into REM sleep, and typically enter into deep sleep during the first third of the night, with higher levels of REM returning during the last period of sleep.

The impact of a poor sleep pattern

A Harvard Medical School survey (2006) on *The Importance of Sleep* highlights that we need sleep for a number of health areas, which will suffer if we have a poor sleep pattern:

- **Learning and memory:** sleep helps the brain take in new information and commit it to memory.

- **Metabolism and weight:** when our body rests, levels of hormones get rebalanced, helping our body to stay healthy.

- **Safety:** sufficient sleep at night means that we are less likely to fall asleep during the day – and possibly have accidents.

SECTION 1

- **Mood:** our mood is negatively impacted by lack of sleep.

- **Cardiovascular health:** it has been shown that stress hormones and heart rate are negatively impacted by lack of sleep.

- **Disease:** the body, when sleep deprived, alters the functioning of the immune system.

The impact of trauma on sleep

There is now a consensus that the term "developmental trauma" (DeRosa et al, 2005) best describes the impact on a child's development caused by abuse and neglect in infancy. A full account of the impact of developmental trauma (which is called in legal terms "significant harm") is comprehensively described in one of the companion books in this series: *Parenting a Child with Emotional and Behavioural Difficulties* (Hughes, 2013). A key issue is the impact of developmental trauma on sleep.

In a review of sleep research (Kajeepeta et al, 2015), the authors found that there was a very clear link between adverse childhood experiences (ACEs) and child and adult sleep disorders. They produced compelling evidence that trauma in childhood not only impacts on sleep patterns in childhood, but that the effect can persist throughout adulthood, if not addressed. The corollary of this is that not only are sleep patterns affected, but they in turn have a marked impact on physical and mental well-being in childhood and into adulthood.

An earlier piece of research (Armstrong et al, 2003), which is of particular relevance for children who come into the care system and who are fostered or subsequently adopted, showed that there is evidence that the origins of problematic childhood sleep behaviour may lie in maternal difficulties and stress during pregnancy and/or levels of maternal stress and depression post birth.

Infants and children with neuro-typical development can, and do, have their sleep patterns managed, largely by behavioural approaches that you see commonly propagated in "Super Nanny" type books and TV programmes. However, for children who are looked after, fostered, in special guardianship families or adopted, sleep is not an attribute of child development that just needs to be managed into a neuro-typical pattern. It is one aspect, along with many other aspects of child development, that requires genuine developmental re-parenting, or therapeutic parenting, on the part of the new family. In a summary of research into adoptive parenting (Ottaway and Selwyn, 2016), the authors offer the following definition of therapeutic re-parenting:

Therapeutic parenting is a deeply nurturing parenting style, with a foundation of self-awareness and a central core of mentalisation, developed from consistent, empathic, insight responses to a child's distress and behaviours: allowing the child to begin to self-regulate, develop an understanding of their own behaviours and ultimately to form secure attachments.

The role of foster carers and adopters is to see sleeping difficulties in this context as something that requires a developmental re-parenting approach to help their child. Kajeepeta *et al* (2015) concluded that it was important for children from traumatic backgrounds, that carers, parents and professionals **treat the trauma and not just the sleep disorder**. The rest of this section will suggest how foster carers and adoptive parents can do this, as part of a holistic approach based on the most up-to-date research into the impact of trauma on child development (McCullough et al, 2016; Vaughan et al, 2016; McCullough et al, 2019). This treatment model is called "Neuro-Physiological Psychotherapy" (NPP). But before thinking further about the impact of trauma on sleep, we first of all need to think about usual sleep practices and good sleep hygiene.

Cultural issues

There are different cultural approaches to how, when and where children should sleep, which may have impacted on children's sleep patterns prior to placement. However, all cultures would see children not sleeping or waking distressed as concerning. New families will need to be aware of any cultural differences between how the child may have been expected to sleep in their previous family and how the adopters or carers would expect the child to sleep, and introduce any changes slowly and sensitively.

Age-related considerations

Infants from four–six months old can potentially sleep through the night, but this can be variable, and depending on the infant, the age at which they achieve this can range from four months to well over a year. This ability to sleep through the night is linked to the infant's ability to eat sufficient solid food to sustain them. However, with a population of children who have had poor parenting prior to placement, parents and carers may have to take a step back developmentally, and first of all help the child make the transition from liquid to solid food with nutritional value, which may delay the timeframe for the child sleeping through the night.

Good sleep hygiene

The overarching advice in relation to sleep for all children is that **routine and consistency are key**. Though we fully appreciate that achieving this is, or can be, difficult for children who have come into the care system and have been traumatised, it is useful to bear this basic advice in mind.

- Stick to the same bedtime for the child, even at weekends.

- Give the child the message that beds are for sleeping and not for games, and importantly when thinking about traumatised children, that the bedroom is a safe place.

- Beds and bedrooms should be cosy, comforting and safe environments.

- Alarm clocks, if used, are for waking up and not for watching, and should be unobtrusive in the room.

- The child's bedtime routines should be predictable.

- Pre-bedtime activities should be quiet, calm and relaxing.

- Children should be helped to relax through touch and body-based interventions as part of a bedtime routine – we provide more information and ideas for this later.

- Starting the day with exercise helps children to use pent-up energy.

- If older children can't sleep, they can read a book or do something calming, but should not use digital screens, e.g. tablets and mobile phones.

- Children should be put to bed when they are drowsy but still awake.

- Children should be encouraged to cuddle up with a soft toy or blanket or other transitional object – we provide more information and ideas about this later.

SECTION 1

- Bedtime check-ups should be short and sweet – just long enough to convey to the child that parents/carers are ensuring they are safe and OK.

- If the child has sleep issues, it is helpful for parents/carers to maintain a sleep diary for their child so that patterns can be detected.

Of course, all this is not straightforward if children in their birth family or in previous foster families have not been used to a predictable routine, or if early experiences have taught them that night-times are not safe. When it comes to bedtime, these children may be unable to settle and become increasingly anxious. The challenge is to work out how good sleep hygiene can be achieved, but it may need to be adjusted or rethought in the light of our understanding of developmental trauma and how the brain has evolved.

CHAPTER 2

A neuro-physiological approach to sleep

Neuro-physiological and neuro-sequential may be unfamiliar concepts to many readers, and may not seem immediately meaningful when thinking about sleep difficulties. In a nutshell, what they refer to is the architecture of the brain.

Neuro-physiological approach

This relates to the actual, physical structure of the brain, and what different parts do. There are three parts to the structure of the brain, which reflect how it has evolved.

- The first and oldest part of the brain has been called the "**primitive brain**" or "**reptilian brain**", and controls life support functions and our fear response. This part of the brain oversees our body temperature, heart rate and breathing; this physiological regulation is fundamental to thinking about sleep.

- The second structure is the "**limbic brain**", which, amongst other things is responsible for processing feelings and memory. It is also the part of the brain that relates to others and helps us to develop relationships. It is these relationships that can support, or in some cases sadly not support, children trying to calm the primitive brain.

- The third structure is the **cortex** or "**thinking brain**", which is responsible for problem solving and being able to reflect and make sense of both the internal and external world.

To focus on sleep, one needs to be **physiologically calm** (primitive brain), and in a **safe relationship** (limbic brain), in order to be able to put in place this higher brain **reflective thinking and meaning making** (cortex).

The different parts of the brain are important in the context of sleep because it is pointless telling a child to calm down when they are being controlled by their primitive brain – particularly if you have been exasperated and there is a hint of anger or threat in your voice. It is the child's primitive brain that is physiologically driving their behaviour, and it is likely to be further activated by an angry, or in any way frustrated, parent. Instead, parents and carers need to first turn their attention and focus to the child's body and their physiological dis-regulation. The parents' or carers' role is to become the thinking brain for the child and problem-solve what it is that is triggering the child's primitive brain, because the child will probably not be able to know or articulate what is upsetting them.

Neuro-sequential approach

This simply means that you have to follow the neurological and developmental pattern and calm the child's primitive brain, getting into a safe attachment relationship, and only then begin to think and talk about the problem (the sleep issues). So, in other words, always work from the primitive brain upwards to the higher brain – parenting from back to front.

A hypothetical example of this would be for you to imagine yourself to be driving on a motorway late at night in poor weather, and your car breaks down. There will be the inevitable feeling of panic and anxiety, but probably you will use your mobile phone to ring a friend to tell them of your predicament, and they will use their calm, reflective capacity to suggest you ring a breakdown service or the police. However, if you are a traumatised individual, you will not only be overwhelmed by panic and anxiety, but by feelings of helplessness and shame, which could prevent you from ringing a friend who could provide that calm, reflective response and problem-solving ability. This is the situation that many traumatised children find themselves in on a day-to-day basis. They are perpetually stuck on a motorway, in the dark, with no help on the way because they are locked into a state of fear and do not have the capacity, or trust, to use another person to help them get off the road!

In the last 15 years, neuro-scientific research has transformed our thinking about psychology, psychotherapy and psychiatry. Sleep difficulties, along with many other childhood challenges and disorders, have, in the past, been managed by professionals using either a psychoanalytic or behaviour modification approach. **But what neuroscience has taught us is that when looking at child development, we need a more holistic approach that encompasses the biological, neurological and psychological aspects in an integrated way. This is the basis of the neuro-physiological psychotherapy (NPP) approach, in this instance, to sleep difficulties.**

Survival mode

If a child is still traumatised when placed in a new family, it means that they are at times still actively operating in a "fight, flight or freeze" survival mode based in the primitive brain. The NPP approach tells us a great deal about the degree to which they are in survival mode and therefore physiologically highly stressed and unable to be calm and to feel safe. A child may have been in foster care managing reasonably well, but the move to another family is highly likely to trigger their nervous system back into a "fight, flight or freeze" response.

When in this state, sleep is hard to achieve, as the body is physiologically wired to be on alert and ready for action. For some children, this might mean it is hard to relax and sleep, as they are hyper-aroused, especially if "bad things" have happened at night in the past. For other children, it might mean that they don't drift off to sleep, but quite literally pass out into a dissociative unconscious state – this is another way of coping with nocturnal anxiety and fear. **Alertness or a shut-down response are both survival states and both outside the conscious control of the child.**

If the child has not yet learned that their new world, their new family, and the adults in it are safe, then their body will continue to be wired in the ways that they used to survive their past traumatic experiences. This means that it is going to be really hard for them to calm and settle into sleep in the usual "sleep hygiene" way. Every cell in their body will be sounding the alarm. We survive trauma by having such alarm systems in the brain and body. Shutting these systems down once they are activated is not easy.

It is not just children's brains that are wired for trauma, but also their hormones. When primitive brain "fight, flight or freeze" responses are triggered, so too are adrenaline secretions. When adrenal secretion is high, melatonin secretion (a hormone necessary for sound sleep), is low. The interrelationship between trauma, melatonin production and sleep underpins the rationale for a lot of sleep strategies. Dr Richard Ferber's book on sleep (2013) is very comprehensive and deals with sleep at this neuro-biological level.

We believe a neuro-biological approach and an understanding of trauma are important in order to be able to relax and soothe a child – particularly a child who has been affected by trauma and loss in their early life. First, we need to think about how to calm the child's body. This body calming is of course not just necessary at night-time, but also during the day, and the first step to parenting any traumatised child is to think about helping them to regulate their feeling states. Sadly, for many fostered and adopted children, night-times can be particularly linked to early trauma and a time of day when scary or unpredictable things happened.

CASE STUDY

During a therapy session with **Linda (six years old)**, her response to the door clicking open was huge, sending her in that moment into a fear state, clearly terrified about what the door click might mean. The noise of the door, we later learned, was associated for Linda with her grandfather entering her room prior to abusing her. This example highlights how little it can take for a child's nervous system to be activated. Even infants will have learned to orientate to the world of their first families. In their birth families, there was perhaps no predictable pattern, no regular bedtime routine, maybe even no bed and no safe adult to tuck them in.

Trauma, sadly, does not always end with a good permanent placement. The very process of coming into care and being looked after is traumatic. When children are removed from a potentially harmful environment, they have no way of understanding what may come next. They may also experience moves from emergency placements to short-term placements, respite care and sometimes failed placements. A history of multiple placements will leave a child trapped in fear and uncertainty about carers and their future. This sense of confusion and fragmentation is not helped when information about the child's history is not shared with their current carer, who is therefore unable to help the child make sense of their history. Even when that history is known, carers and adoptive parents are often fearful of referring to it as they don't wish to distress or upset their child, and because they are often themselves upset and distressed by the information. Any parent or carer in this position should ask for professional guidance and assistance from a social worker or therapist as to how best to make sense of troubling information for themselves and their child.

How to calm a child operating in "survival mode"

To begin physiologically, one needs to think about how to create a safe bedroom and help the child orientate to the new family and new bedroom that they are now being asked to relax and go to sleep in.

Children who have been traumatised orientate to the world around them with eyes that have a "trauma lens", so that what they see is driven by a nervous system that has been wired to survive their early traumatic experiences. Humans usually manage most of the time to keep in balance the information they gather from the world around them (extroceptive information) with the internal information they receive about how they are feeling (introceptive information). So if we hear a door bang and our body jolts, we can recognise that it is a door banging and not a fight starting; the information both externally and internally makes sense and our body does not get triggered into "fight, flight or freeze". However, if you are a child who has been traumatised in the past, the door banging can trigger panic, with the child's whole body becoming activated. Similarly, and importantly, if a child has learned early in life that scary things happen at night, adults fight, get drunk and sometimes come into your bedroom and abuse you, then when the lights go off, even the shadow of their dressing gown can be enough to trigger a fear response. They most likely will not even know that this is what is happening, as their fear response is so wired into their system.

We know that trauma causes us to "orientate" differently to the world, and take in all the external information with heightened senses to scan for danger. The body simply does not calm, but continues to scan the environment for trauma even when the situation has changed. In essence, the child is so primed to have heightened orientating skills, and so wired to trauma, that they are quite literally reading the world around them inaccurately. The first step towards helping your child to sleep is helping them to use their senses to orientate to the *actual* world around them, rather than to the perceived threat they are so used to scanning the environment for, so that the internal and external information begin to match up. This is going to take time and support, as it is not an easy process to calm the child's nervous system. Steps three and four in the next chapter explore this.

The other key issue to take into account is that the trauma for most children who have come from the care system is **relational**. By this, we mean that the trauma is related to relationships, and may therefore leave children finding people scary. A child with this relational trauma will need to re-learn how to use their parent or carer to support them in calming themselves and going to sleep. This is no mean feat if the child has historically learned that adults can be the source of fear, and that even an adult who at times can be kind, may also be unpredictable and ultimately cannot be trusted. So parents and carers need to be mindful that their proximity to the child may be confusing at best, and terrifying at worst; their very presence could even inhibit the child's ability to sleep. This is complicated, and the role of the parent or carer in supporting the child to ease into sleep will be discussed in more detail in the next chapter.

CHAPTER 3

Taking steps to help your child sleep well

General principles for children who have been, or are, in care

Whether it is as a result of neglect, abuse and/or multiple placements, your child's neuro-physiological and psychological systems will have become wired to cope with fear in all its manifestations. Returning to our mantra of "going back in order to go forward", as most sleep problems have their origins in infancy, the parent or carer trying to manage them should respond as one would to a young infant. But whilst parenting a baby requires attuned and soothing parenting strategies, parenting a traumatised baby is more complex because you must not only be aware of, but also understand their first experiences.

The focus for parents with children who have sleep difficulties must be on **regulation** (primitive brain) and **attachment** (limbic brain). Life story work and making sense of the past, as well as problem solving, require higher brain (cortex) thinking and so are harder to access for lots of children who are still stuck in "'fight, flight or freeze" mode. For **Joshua** (five years old), whose history involved being locked in a cupboard, hearing doors being slammed and shouting, meant that he found a dark bedroom terrifying and needed both a night light and his adoptive mother's voice playing on a tape in the background to reassure him that he was safe. So, in parenting a traumatised child with sleep difficulties, one has to be aware of the general principles of parenting a traumatised child, together with that child's specific trauma history. It is this history that will inform the details of the neuro-physiological strategies for resolving sleep difficulties that we outline below.

Step 1: Developmental assessment

All children who have been in the care system should have a comprehensive developmental assessment. This is because it is now recognised that there is a high incidence or possibility of the following conditions:

- developmental trauma

- Sensory Processing Disorder (SPD) or difficulties

- Foetal Alcohol Spectrum Disorder (FASD)

- Autism Spectrum Disorder (ASD)

- Attention Deficit Hyperactivity Disorder (ADHD)

The first two conditions (developmental trauma and Sensory Processing Disorder) are most common in our clinical experience, but the other three also need to be considered, as there is a high incidence in children from the care system. All of these conditions interfere with healthy sleep patterns. Whether a child is suffering from one or more of these conditions (co-morbidity), an accurate diagnosis is a first step towards ensuring that appropriate support and funding are available, and appropriate strategies for home and school are in place to help the child to achieve their potential.

In relation to Sensory Processing Disorder and difficulties, it may be that a specific Sensory Integration Assessment would be helpful. We look at possible sensory integration-based strategies for children's sleep problems later in this chapter.

Another area to bear in mind is the connection between nutrition and poor sleep. There is growing evidence that vitamin and mineral deficiencies can impair the quality of our sleep (Hookway, 2019). A nutritional assessment should be a part of any assessment, as a child may be moved from a nutrition-poor to a nutrition-rich placement, and their capacity to absorb and utilise the extra nutrition will often be impaired.

The first step towards thinking about your child's sleep difficulties is to understand your child's history of abuse and neglect and make some educated guesses about the origins of their fears and fantasies about going to sleep. Sleep for the traumatised child is experienced as a state of vulnerability in a hostile environment.

Step 2: Understand your child's sleep history

You may be able to find out about your child's sleep history from their previous foster carers, or from your social worker. Then consider their probably different sleep pattern in their birth family and/or previous foster family, and how they are managing sleep now. How far is their sleep pattern now a reflection of their history, and does their sleep have a dissociative "shut down" feel, or is it in alert survival mode? We have seen some children

21

who sleep so lightly that they immediately wake at the slightest disturbance or even sleep with their eyes open. We have also seen children who sleep so deeply that nothing will wake them. Neither of these are healthy, normal sleep patterns.

If children are old enough, above the age of four or five, and able to have a relaxed conversation about their early life experiences, and sleep as a part of these, it can be helpful for you to explain to the child why they are fearful at night, in order to give them some context for their feelings and to help them make sense of what is happening. (It is best not to attempt this at bedtime, but at another time of the day.) This will help the child not to feel guilty, blamed or shamed for their difficulties around sleep. It will also give you a framework to refer to when a child is experiencing difficulties at night. We cannot stress enough how important this step is; it differentiates sleep strategies between the traumatised and the non-traumatised child. Purely addressing current behaviours, in our experience, ultimately does not work with traumatised children.

CASE STUDY

Troy (aged 10) would often become extremely angry at bedtime with his adoptive mother trying to put him to bed, and this could go on for hours. When seen in the context of Troy's history, his behaviour made perfect sense. Troy was expressing his anger at the way he had been treated at bedtime in his birth family, albeit projecting it onto his adoptive mother. He was also stalling the imminent bedtime that he associated with being trapped in his room. When looking at Troy's history with him, it was apparent that every night in the birth family, he had been locked in a dark room to sleep on a cold, damp mattress. When in the room, he could see very little but he could hear his birth parents and others arguing, shouting, and fighting, leaving him feeling scared and helpless. His adoptive mother and a therapist were able to help Troy draw a picture of this dark and scary "bedroom", and discuss with him how normal it would be to feel scared, rejected and angry in this situation – how it should never have happened to him, it was not his fault that he was shut in, and it was not because he was bad in any way, but because his birth parents didn't look after him. By being helped to articulate his experience and externalise it by drawing it, Troy was able to see that his traumas were in the past, not the present, that his fears and fantasies around sleep needed to change as his life experience had now changed. This process also helped his adoptive mother to understand Troy and his behaviour better, and if Troy "acted out" at bedtime, she was able to be empathic and attuned to Troy's feeling state.

Children who have come into the care system, for whatever reason, and have experienced moves and losses, will be on a continuum of traumatic life experiences, which will continue to have an impact on their behaviour if they are not dealt with appropriately. Trauma is a subjective experience and the impact on each child will be different, with some children being more resilient than others.

Step 3: Think about your child's bedtime routine

Think about your child's bedtime routine and whether it provides sufficient calm and gentle easing into a sleep state. Warm baths, bedtime stories, massage, soothing music, soft lights, and no screen time before bed are all part of sleep hygiene good practice. Consider how much your child, when supposedly going to sleep, is not actually orientating to the real environment of your home but is on alert in relation to their past. Can you help by encouraging your child to use their senses to really notice the home environment and their bedroom and relationships within this home? Take time to check what you and they can see, or what noises they can hear in the rest of the home. This process of re-orientating to the real environment and encouraging the child to connect internal information with the external world is key to helping calm their nervous system. Parents and carers need to think "body" and think "nervous system". So, consider:

- your child's heart rate;

- your child's breathing;

- your child's skin temperature.

You may also want to track your own nervous system and note how your own heart rate, breathing and skin temperature are being activated. If you can regulate yourself, you will be more able to help regulate your child. This is called **co-regulation**. The focus of the regulation needs to be first of all on your child's body so that they are physiologically able to relax. If your child's muscles are pumped up ready for fight or flight, their body physiologically cannot be calm, and they will not be able to fall asleep. So muscles also need to be relaxed, or as much as possible, and the whole physical state of the body calmed.

This calm state can be achieved in various ways:

- It is important to know that the blue light emitted from the screens of computers, tablets and mobile phones has been shown to lower melatonin levels (melatonin is a necessary hormone for sleep), and we therefore suggest no screens prior to the bedtime routine.

- Notice what is happening in your child's body and turn their attention to their fast heart rate and breathing. You can put the child against your heart to help them regulate their own heart.

- Notice what is happening in your own body if you are feeling stressed by the situation as an indicator of what the child may be experiencing.

- It may be helpful to give your child a warm bath with lavender oil, as that is known to have a calming and soothing effect.

- You may need to open a window or get your child a cold drink if they are is too hot, or a warmer blanket or warm drink if they are too cold. Herbal teas such as camomile or valerian can be calming, if your child will drink them. Dairy products and oats contain tryptophan, an amino acid that aids sleep, so a drink of milk or oat milk could be helpful.

- A child who over-heats at night may appreciate bed linen made of a cooling material, or a "cooling pad" on the mattress.

- Orientating to the room is important: make sure that your child is using all their senses to hear, smell, see and touch all their surroundings accurately in the here and now.

- The olfactory or smell sensory system is our primary system for survival and is over-developed in many traumatised children. Providing the child with something such as a pillow, scarf or shirt that is impregnated with the parent's or carer's natural scent can provide a powerful, safe and relational intervention for a scared child.

- Sleeping in a "tent" placed over the bed can provide a safe space for some children, and can help them to calm by reducing their levels of sensory input.

- Work out with your child where you need to be in the room so that the distance between you is not threatening for them and they feel comfortable with it.

- It is not about there being a right or wrong way to help calm your child, but about drawing your child's mind to their body, so that they have some sense of agency over their body and so that they can reach a balance between extroceptive (exterior) and introceptive (interior) information.

- Encourage your child to use a happy memory or image to help them regulate and to calm themselves.

- If your child is comfortable with touch, it may be helpful to use physical contact, such as a firm hand on their back to give some deep pressure touch.

- For some children, massage of agreed parts of the body, that is not too stimulating, can help the body to calm, but this will not be an option for children who have difficulties with touch.

- For some children, gentle pressure on the body covered by a blanket or duvet can help them to calm.

- For some children, your voice singing or telling them a story in a rhythmic and low tone can help them to calm.

- For some children, ambient sounds playing in the background can be reassuring and help them to calm.

The pre-sleep state

At bedtime, some children may want to engage you in discussions about distressing things that have happened to them, often in the past. It is of course really important to listen, and to acknowledge their wish to share their past history with you, but there is also a point when the discussions need to be put to one side and quite literally filed away in the brain. The child in this pre-sleep state is having more access to their worries, and hence their history and unconscious memories come to the surface. As the parent or carer, you have to work out when to say that these things are all really important to think about the next day, and you will help them to remember then. Children may find it helpful to have a box or container in which these important memories or worries can be stored to be looked at the following day or in a therapy session. The brain stores memories too, but sometimes, perhaps most of all when these memories are too distressing, it is as if there is no space in the brain's filing cabinet, and these memories float around in the child's unconscious mind until they can be filed. As the parent or carer supporting the child, you can offer containment and a way of helping your child to manage their unmanageable feelings and worries. Later the following day or week, these important issues can be reviewed by you and your child together.

Step 4: Help your child to feel safe at night

Experiment with different ways of supporting your child to feel safe at night, with nightlights, the door open, your voice on an audio device, etc. Think sensory, and support the child's sensory system to become calm. It is not only the child's trauma history that can disrupt sleep, but also the child's ability, or inability, to regulate their sensory system. If children have been traumatised and had poor parenting in infancy, their capacity to process sensory information and to manage their sensory system has often been impaired and distorted. Supporting the sensory system of these children is essential to help them manage in the day, but also at night.

27

Specific sensory integration strategies to facilitate sleep

Children who have additional sensory integration difficulties may well struggle with sleep. Children who seek a lot of movement at bedtime may have an under-responsive (hypo-reactive) sensory system. These children settle better after activity in the early evening that provides additional input, such as walking the dog, or doing forward rolls across the floor, or being rolled up (swaddled) in a blanket and gently rocked. Some children are more extreme in their need for sensory input to regulate their nervous system, and will require a planned play session in the late afternoon, which should include intense sensory input.

Children who are "sensory defensive" and appear agitated or fussy at bedtime may be finding that their environment is bothering their visual, auditory and tactile systems so that they cannot get comfortable. The following suggestions are sensory strategies that can be considered to help with this:

- "white noise" or calming music to modulate background noise;

- black-out blinds or an eye mask to block out light;

- applying "deep tactile pressure" techniques, such as a firm hand or back massage, or a "weighted blanket" can be considered, especially for getting off to sleep.

- sleeping in a sleeping bag; some children like the safety of the additional deep pressure squeeze from adding pillows to the bag.
  A note of warning: pressure techniques are not safe or suitable for infants.

Step 5: Consider your child's attachment relationships

Be aware of the complexity, for your child, of their attachment relationships. How can you help them to know that you are a safe and to-be-trusted adult? It is not possible for a child to use their attachment figure (you) to help them drift off to sleep, if adults are still perceived to be a source of fear. It is, of course, also important to be bear in mind that many children generally feel that they can trust their new parent (their secure base), but at times of heightened stress this sense of safety can disappear. It may therefore be that your child is less able to access you as their secure base at night-time when stress responses are more likely to be triggered.

Many fostered and adopted children have what is considered to be "disorganised" attachments, meaning that their attachment strategies are not necessarily organised or consistent, and at times of stress their more disorganised strategies will come to the fore. They will oscillate between fearful, controlling, angry and avoidant strategies, making it hard to understand them, and even harder to support them. Dan Hughes (2013) writes about developmental trauma disorder, a symptom of which is attachment disorder:

> …avoidant, anxious, and especially disorganised patterns make it difficult for the child to seek comfort and support, accept guidance and direction, communicate openly, develop the sense of safety necessary to explore the world and develop autonomy.

If you can achieve a state of calm and regulation of the child's primitive brain, then your child will be free to allow themselves to

29

SECTION I

feel secure and safe in a caring attachment relationship with you, which is the precursor to allowing you to support them in going to sleep. The calming of the primitive brain and the development of an attachment relationship in the limbic brain are interrelated and co-dependant on one another.

One of the positive results of establishing a healthy sleep pattern is that it becomes part of the basis of forming a good attachment relationship with your child, which generalises beyond sleep into day-to-day interactions.

Step 6: Talk about the problem with your child

Talk to your child at other times than during bed and night-times about their problems with going to sleep or staying asleep. This reflective process would involve helping them to see the links between their early history and their current difficulties. It is important not to push your child to talk if they resist or feel overwhelmed by this sort of discussion. It would only be helpful if the child is willing to tease out with you why things are the way they are and what might help to make them better. This could be an issue explored with you and the child together making sense of sleep difficulties with the help of a dyadic therapist. [1]

In many ways, this is like a life story work approach, and all part of helping you and your child together to think about their history and origins. It requires the child and the parent or carer to be in a calm, regulated state and relating to each other, so that

---

[1] Dyadic Developmental Psychotherapy (DDP) is a psychotherapeutic treatment method for families that have children with symptoms of emotional disorders, including complex trauma and attachment disorders. It was originally developed by Dan Hughes.

higher brain reflective thinking is possible without the child being triggered into a trauma state.

This higher stage of brain function is not just an attribute of older children; it is a capacity that children of all ages have when they are in an optimal, quiet but alert state. Parents and carers, perhaps with some assistance, need to find the right age- and stage-appropriate words to discuss distressing life events and why they may be hindering the child's sleep. It is also important to be mindful that just because a child can reflect on their sleep difficulties when they are calm during the day, this does not mean that they can access this higher brain thinking when they become stressed at bedtime. It is a slow and gradual process, and just understanding why, does not necessarily or immediately solve the problem. However, it provides a framework, which over time can generate a meaningful dialogue between parent and child, as it did for Troy and his parent in the earlier case study.

CHAPTER **4**

Adapting Theraplay strategies to help sleep

Theraplay is a dyadic therapy (dyadic means the interaction between two things) that works with parent and child together to address behavioural, emotional and developmental issues to improve the parent–child relationship through play and healthy interaction.

It is helpful at this point to think about the four domains that Theraplay (2009) uses in therapy for parents and children together, as these domains are pertinent both to good parenting and attachment forming behaviour that one needs to think about in relation to sleep. The four domains are:

- structure;

- nurture;

- engagement; and

- challenge.

Structure

It is good to think about the structure of the day and night-time for your child. If there has been a move from another family to your family, a good and sensible structure around sleep and day-time naps may or may not be in place, and can easily be upset by the transition. It is helpful when considering your child's sleep difficulties to keep a diary of their sleep at night and naps during the day so that you build up a clear picture of the patterns and can then think strategically about what needs to change and how to change it:

- What is your child's bedtime routine?

- What time does your child go to bed?

- Does your child settle instantly or does it take hours?

- Do you stay with your child or nearby until they go to sleep?

- Does your child wake in the night?

- What time does your child wake in the morning?

- How many naps does your child have in the day?

- If your child drifts off in the car or elsewhere at the end of the day, is it more difficult for them to settle at night?

- Is your day and night structure regular, or does it frequently change due to external factors such as work patterns?

Analysing and reviewing the structure that you are trying to put in place and assessing the connection between night-time patterns and day-time activities is key to making sense of what you can do practically to help your child sleep well. A good routine and rituals around bedtimes as well as consistency will make a big difference to a child's sleep pattern.

It is not advisable for digital devices, which can stimulate the brain in a non-sleep receptive way, to be left unsupervised with your child. If you are already doing this, or the child was using digital devices prior to placement with you, it is best to work in incremental stages to remove a device. There may, however, be times when it is advisable to put a ban on devices and survive the intense distress that will likely ensue – as it would hopefully be short term. A dependence on devices is really sustaining a false sense of autonomy rather than attending to the real issue of learning to trust and be dependent and use parents or carers to reduce anxiety.

Sleep does not begin at bedtime but in the hours or even the day leading up to bedtime. Earlier in the day, the child may need to have a lot of physical activity to calm and regulate their nervous system; time out of doors, getting fresh air, will be important to include in your structure. As the day moves towards evening, food and bath time routines become important preparation for the bedtime ritual of stories, songs and good night hugs.

Nurture

Nurture may not be easy to accept for a child with a traumatic history. How you plan to nurture your child and comfort them at bedtimes will have to be creative. Some children are clingy and needy at night and find it hard to separate; it is vital for your child to learn to manage separation. If children already have separation anxiety, it may be particularly evident at night-time. In the longer term, it is not a good idea if your child is only able to settle if you are present until they drift off to sleep. It may well mean that they wake later in the night in a panic when you are not there.

Your child needs ultimately to learn that they can be safe in bed, and that when you leave the room they are not abandoned and in danger but can feel safe enough to relax into sleep.

Enabling a traumatised child with attachment difficulties to trust you to leave the room can be very hard. It may need to be broken down into stages, so that you begin near the bed and move gradually nearer to the door, then wait outside the room, maybe humming a tune the child likes, and finally engaging in a domestic activity that the child can hear and recognise. It may be that a child needs your scarf/t-shirt with your natural scent, or a distinctive perfume or aftershave on it as a transitional object to help them settle. Some parents use their voice recording of a story they have read before to help their child feel that they are present.

The avoidant child, who finds intimacy, nurture and touch at bedtimes hard, and is not yet sure what a parent is really there for, may still need you to offer them your scarf/t-shirt and your time and attention. However, be aware that the proximity of an adult at bedtime may have to be worked up to. It may be that the goodnight cuddle and kiss has to be a butterfly kiss (eyelashes on cheek) or an elephant trunk kiss (arm as trunk and suction sound as end of arm trunk touches cheek gently) or other ways of your own, showing that you love and care for the child. Start at a distance that the child can tolerate and then move closer, rather than starting where you would like to be.

Nurture, touch and intimacy are essential for children's healthy development and their immune system. It is natural for parents when putting their children to bed to use touch, but sadly children with difficult early experiences may not be used to this sort of parental nurture and their touch sensors have often been damaged, so that they can experience touch as potentially painful or anxiety provoking. It is going to take time, and you may have to take small steps to make touch acceptable.

It is important to set all the strategies in context for the child. You may want to say something like: 'In this family, this is how we show our love and affection for you'. Acknowledge that this may not have been the child's previous experience but that you want to make it feel good and safe for them. So along with the strategy, there will need to be a narrative, even for quite young children. Sometimes words do not help and it is more the sound and tone of the voice that is key. Think about calming the child's primitive brain with your voice, using a melodic tone that soothes and has rhythm. You don't want to hypnotise your child to sleep, but you can use your voice to soothe them.

It is also important to think about food in relation to sleep and nurture. If your child was put to bed hungry in their birth family, you may have to address this by offering them food at bedtime. A hungry child will not sleep, and just a bedtime drink of warm milk may actually help. If your child either struggles to eat or is constantly hungry, you may need to think about this too, as sore tummies with too much food, as well as empty tummies rumbling with hunger, or upset tummies with constipation, will all be a problem. Again, it is helpful to explain why you are doing this, so that your child knows you are nurturing them, and realises that you understand their early experiences.

Children who have suffered early trauma may have problems with blood sugar level balance or may have been so poorly fed that their preference for sweet and fatty foods means that they don't have enough protein to sustain them during the night. Your child may or may not like warm milk, but something to eat or drink to help them manage all night without another meal is going to be important. If they have other issues related to food, further investigation and consideration may be required.

It is also important to think about the sensory environment for the child at bedtime. Is lighting an issue? Does your child

need a night light or an open door with a light on in the hall?
A comfortable bed and cushions, sleep inducing smells such as
lavender (although this is not for everyone) and maybe sticking
glow-in-the-dark stars on the ceiling or a picture of a favourite
animal on the wall can soothe and reassure. What you aim to
create is a sensory surrounding of comfort and safety, which is an
important aspect of nurture.

Engagement

Children's sleep difficulties predominantly arise from a sense of
fear and foreboding as to what may happen to them, or around
them, at night if they do not remain alert, because in the past
they have been vulnerable. As many of their fears, conscious or
unconscious, past or present, come from a sense of powerlessness
and loss of control, it is important that your child can feel a sense
of mastery over what happens around bedtimes. Engagement
in this context is really about creating a sense of collaboration
and empowerment for the child. It is important for parents and
carers to see their child's struggle with sleep as a struggle against
fear of the unknown. If you can help your child to regain a sense
of control, a feeling of safety will follow. This is not letting the
child dictate, but giving them some agency over the process, for
example, the choice of story book, or song, or goodnight kiss.
You do, however, need to keep the structure in place, and the
process should not become a battleground that leads to endless
procrastination over more and more stories, or songs, or glasses
of water. Again, go back to their early life experience and help your
child to see that their lack of control has led to fear and anxiety,
but it is not the same in this family now.

Challenge

"Challenge" is the term Theraplay uses to describe appropriate challenges at each developmental stage. It is important to bear in mind when helping children to sleep, that this is a skill most children learn in their infancy, but which children who have had poor parenting may not have learned at all. This can apply to a child of any age, and it is important when it comes to looking at developmental challenges to distinguish between what is age-appropriate behaviour and what is developmental stage-appropriate behaviour. For the majority of traumatised children, there will be a discrepancy between these two measures. Traumatised children will often function at a much younger level than you might expect for their age. They will therefore need parenting that takes this into account.

If children struggle to sleep, parental decisions have to be made about how to manage this challenge by offering a consistent, calm and empathic but clear response. It can help if you think about the sleep difficulties as a developmental stage-related issue rather than an age-related issue. Parents often become more empathic if they see themselves as providing the parenting that was not available when the child was an infant, struggling to learn how to sleep whilst living in adverse conditions.

CHAPTER 5

Frequently asked questions

This chapter sets out clear, practical answers to a number of frequently asked, day-to-day questions about children's sleep issues.

How quickly or slowly should I change the child's sleeping routine from a previous placement?

The general advice for prospective permanent families for children of all ages is to adhere to the practice of the previous carers initially, so that the child does not have to struggle even more with the transition and discontinuity. However, if there are sleep patterns or rituals that are problematic, then they do need to be addressed early on in the new placement using the steps that we have outlined earlier in this guide. It is very stressful for parents of newly placed children if they do not sleep, and ultimately no one in the family sleeps well. The importance of sleep cannot be overestimated and therefore needs to be addressed in ways that are commensurate with developmental re-parenting.

How can I rule out medical reasons for sleep difficulties?

It is always important to rule out possible medical causes. A doctor would expect that good, sensible sleep hygiene rituals are in place, and only if they were confident that the parent or carer was doing all the usual things to help a child sleep would they consider a referral to a specialist paediatrician to investigate other causes of sleep problems, such as sleep apnoea.

If your child has any diagnosed conditions, it would be worth consulting your GP as to whether these conditions are known to have an impact on sleep.

What if the child has issues with bed-wetting?

Bed-wetting can have a huge impact on a child's sleep cycle and the quality of their sleep. The parents' or carers' sleep pattern will also be disrupted by a wet bed that needs changing. It may be necessary, in order to resolve sleep difficulties, to also consider bed-wetting problems. CoramBAAF's book, in this same series, on toileting issues (Fenton, 2019) provides comprehensive information focused on the particular issues for fostered and adopted children. Dr Richard Ferber (2013) devotes a whole chapter of his book on sleep to bed-wetting. He highlights the fact that development of the hormone system affects children's night-time continence. This needs to be taken into account when trying to resolve wetting problems and requires medical advice.

If your child is experiencing bed-wetting as an issue, they will be hyper-sensitive to shame and blame, and may become angry and upset about their powerlessness to resolve the problem. It is therefore a topic that needs the utmost sensitivity and a careful assessment of the causal factors, because a simple behavioural approach could easily tip into an unhelpful and negative experience for a child of feeling not understood and blamed, rather than being helped to make sense of the bed-wetting as part of their trauma history.

Some sleep problems cannot be resolved until bed-wetting is resolved, and bed-wetting, unless there is a medical cause, cannot be resolved until the underlying trauma-based anxiety is lessened. The key is to work out which issue is the one to begin focusing on.

Can melatonin help?

Melatonin is a hormone secreted at the end of the day, and is sometimes known as the "sleep hormone". The production and release of melatonin, from the pineal gland, occurs in a clear daily rhythm, with peak levels at night. Once produced, melatonin is secreted into the bloodstream and fluid around the brain and spinal cord, and conveys signals to distant organs.

Melatonin can be taken as a supplement and used to treat difficulties around going to sleep and staying asleep. It may benefit children who are developing normally, as well as children with Attention Deficit Hyperactivity Disorder (ADHD), autism, other developmental disabilities, or visual impairment.

However, there has been concern expressed in the media about melatonin. For example, Sarah Marsh (*The Guardian*, 29 May 2017) wrote that melatonin is being overused to help children sleep, and can be counterproductive. The important point to remember, as Professor Paul Gringras (a leading expert on sleep) says in the same article, is that:

Children with autism and other developmental problems often don't make enough melatonin at night or produce it too late. That is why it works well for those groups.

He also makes the cautionary point (quite rightly) that:

Melatonin should not be prescribed even for these groups of children where there aren't good bedtime routines in place. It is not a single solution.

Dr Richard Ferber (2013) points out that melatonin does not induce sleep directly, but makes falling asleep easier by tricking the brain into thinking that the sleep phase has already started. He suggests that taking melatonin in the late afternoon might be more effective than waiting until the evening, as it helps to shift the daily sleep cycle to an earlier start. He also advises caution regarding its long-term use, as little is known about side effects in the longer term.

Although melatonin is a natural hormone in the body, as with anything that one ingests, it is important to seek medical advice and a prescription for melatonin rather than buying online, as it needs to be carefully sourced and monitored. What is important for parents and carers is to know that this is something that could be considered for their child, particularly as it is known that trauma and emotional stress in infancy disrupt the daily sleep cycles and produce adrenaline, and adrenaline inhibits melatonin production and release.

Should specific foods be offered/avoided before bedtime?

If a child is hungry it is as hard for them as it would be for an adult to fall sleep. However, for traumatised children, eating may be a way to seek comfort or self-soothe, so they may want food at bedtime as a way of managing stress. It is important to think about what you give your child before they go to sleep, and the old-fashioned idea that warm milk helps us to sleep is actually accurate, because the brain is occupied as it sends blood to the stomach to help the digestion. But if you have a major meal before sleeping, it is not helpful, as lying down on a full stomach can be uncomfortable, cause indigestion and generate too much surplus energy. So really, it is about giving your child something easy to digest that is comforting and not too sugar-based, so that it helps them to feel full and soothed, but not too full.

There are some foods that have been identified as promoting sleep, which include: turkey, bananas, spinach, almonds, cherries, jasmine rice, complex carbohydrates such as oats, sweet potatoes, papaya, kiwi fruit, and, as mentioned above, milk. There are also foods that are stimulating and therefore not good at or near bedtime. These are high fat foods, caffeinated drinks, chocolate, tomatoes, aubergine, refined carbohydrates and sugar, spicy foods, high protein foods, and dried fruit (Hookway, 2019).

Is co-sleeping appropriate for a traumatised child?

There are a couple of cautionary points to be aware of when considering co-sleeping: the danger of allegations if you co-sleep can be high as it may remind your child of abuse; and abuse may have been perpetrated by a woman or mother, not just a man or a father, so all parents and carers need to bear this in mind.

A child who has been sexually abused may want to co-sleep to get back to something that feels familiar and may even be comforting, or was a way of keeping themselves safe. Sadly, it is often not known exactly what a child has experienced in terms of abuse, so you need to make sure that you take appropriate measures for safe care. For example, adults should wear night clothes in bed and not have children climb into bed with them when they, or the child, are naked. Culturally acceptable parent/child boundaries and parameters must be put in place from the start of the placement.

Co-sleeping is lovely with a newborn baby. Being close and having that intimacy and connection helps the baby co-regulate and eases breast-feeding. For children who have not had this experience and for parents who would like this closeness and intimacy with their child, co-sleeping can be a good way of connecting. It needs to be thought about and measures put in place to make it as safe as possible, and your social worker should know this is what you are doing and how you are ensuring it is physically safe, and not triggering bad memories for your child. But sharing a bed with their child is also not for everyone, and some parents understandably need their own bed to be a protected space, so it really is a matter of personal choice and negotiation.

A child's early experiences of neglect and abuse and being left on their own by a parent to sleep may have resulted in the child feeling abandoned and/or terrified. If a child has been used to sharing a cramped space, or even a bed, with several other children, a room of their own may overwhelm them. Sleeping with parents/carers or in their room in a special made-up bed can be vital to help them feel safe and to settle. If a child is very young, it may be an appropriate way to start your sleep strategies.

It can also be used as a temporary measure or special treat

to help calm a child who has woken distressed in the night, or when there has been an incident in the day that you know has profoundly disturbed them. Some parents and carers find that their child struggles at particular times of year or on anniversaries of particular events, such as:

- being taken into care;
- police raids on the birth family;
- time of year when the abuse happened;
- time of year when a specific event happened;
- death or departure of a parent figure or sibling;
- religious or cultural festivals such as Christmas;
- birthdays;
- Hallowe'en and Guy Fawkes Night.

Parents may think about using co-sleeping at these particular times in a planned way, if they know in advance that it is going to be tough for the child without this close proximity at night. But sleeping in the same bed or the same room can also be complex and disturb the parents' or carers' sleep. An end strategy has to be borne in mind.

Families have managed to make the transition from co-sleeping by moving the child from their bed to another bed in the same room, before helping the child to sleep in their own bedroom with a transitional object that smells of a parent or carer.

How safe is it for babies to sleep with parents?

There are many different perspectives about co-sleeping with infants, with passionate views held about the benefits as well as serious concerns about the risks. Those advocating for it stress the value of skin-to-skin contact to reduce anxiety and create close emotional bonds. There are, however, concerns about the risk of Sudden Infant Death Syndrome (SIDS) due to co-sleeping. It is recommended, as SIDS is most likely between the ages of two to four months, that you should not co-sleep with your baby until they are over four months and ideally six months old. You should not co-sleep if you have drunk alcohol or taken any medication, as there is then a risk of your rolling over in your sleep and suffocating the baby. Given that most adoptive placements will not involve very young babies, co-sleeping poses a greater risk of allegation and re-enactment than suffocation.

Why was the child sleeping fine before placement but is now waking frequently?

Some prospective adopters or permanent carers have children placed who apparently slept throughout the night with no problem in their previous foster home, but suddenly start waking several times every night in their new home. It may be that the child needs reassurance that a parent or carer will respond kindly when they are distressed at night. It may well be the first time that they have felt safe enough to test whether an attachment figure will be available. In order to respond to this first overture of need, an attempt to control the child's crying would be the antithesis of therapeutic parenting.

It may appear to be a paradox that the child who previously slept through the night in fearful silence, or as an escape from reality, now feels sufficiently safe to demand comfort and reassurance. Parents and carers should see it as a positive step rather than a negative regression. Of course, this is easy to write, but hard to do when one is tired and stressed by lack of sleep as a consequence of this developmental shift. But as for children and infants who find it hard to go to sleep, a developmental approach of "going back in order to go forward" and helping the child to learn the basics of good sleep hygiene is the best approach.

What are night-time fears or terrors?

Dr Richard Ferber (2013) devotes a chapter to night-time fears, which can resurface for a range of reasons even if children have not experienced ongoing trauma. Their fears will not just be anxieties stemming from daily life, but may also be rooted in past reality. This is why night fears for traumatised children need to be addressed as part of a programme of life story work, which will help the child to become aware of the origins of their fears, in order to process them as something that was in the past. Children waking with night terrors can be frightening for parents as well as for the child, but it has been said wisely that what is "shareable is bearable".

There is research evidence, and our clinical experience has shown, that melatonin supplements (discussed above) are helpful in treating night terrors. We also know of parents using the antihistamine medication Piriton, at the suggestion of their GP, to help subdue, and even eradicate, night terrors. We would strongly recommend that these medications be used only under medical supervision.

Is controlled crying appropriate for traumatised infants?

A commonly recommended approach to manage sleep difficulties is to use controlled crying. The baby is put to sleep following the bedtime ritual, and if they cry as soon as they are left, rather than going back immediately to comfort them, the parent is encouraged to leave them to cry for short periods, only returning at specific intervals to settle them with minimal words and quiet, clear messages that now is the time to sleep. If the child wakes in the night, the same process is followed. For a baby without a trauma history, there is a clear rationale for this method. If it is done calmly and sensibly, it can work well. It is stressful for the parents, but generally in a few days it can resolve the crying and waking up pattern and support a baby in learning to go to sleep without the parent present.

The question is: how does this apply to traumatised infants whose experiences of abandonment and terror are very real? A behavioural controlled crying approach, if sensitively done, can still be appropriate and effective. If you are going to try controlled crying, it would be advisable not to leave long gaps before returning to reassure the baby, so that whilst the norm for other infants may be to leave longer gaps, for a traumatised infant one would be thinking of starting with three or four minute gaps. We would still discourage much talking; a touch on the back and comforting phrase such as: 'It is OK, I am here and you are safe' would be sufficient. Importantly, you need to be consistent and stick with it, but also know the point at which your child's distress is more than it is reasonable to allow. It is probably best to seek professional support and advice about how to manage controlled crying because this approach can risk re-traumatising a child by giving them the message that their new parents or carers are neglectful, which may resonate with unconscious memories of infancy and the sheer terror of abandonment.

Again, it is important to know the infant's history, and if the night time care is not documented, parents, carers and professionals have to use their creative intelligence to speculate that if the infant was left with very young carers or had birth parents who were substance misusers, it is likely that their night-time waking and cries would not have elicited a response.

Can a child sleep too much?

Sometimes children, in response to trauma and stress, can find that sleep provides them with a perfect way of literally blanking out the world and all their stress and anxiety. Sleep then becomes more of a dissociative state and a "freeze" response to stress, and it is hard for them to wake up. But sometimes children just need more sleep, so it is worth considering if they need an earlier bedtime.

If your child has trouble waking in the morning, it would be good to review their whole sleep routine and sleep cycle. Are they managing to go to bed and drift off to sleep, and move through different sleep stages? If they are not, but the moment their head hits the pillow they are asleep, then you know that it is not just waking that is the problem, but their sleep as a whole. Waking a heavily sleeping child is hard and requires sensitivity and a gradual approach, as you are not waking a child only from sleep, but from a dissociative state.

Children who find it hard to wake in the morning need the same sorts of strategies as are used to help children get off to sleep. You need to allow more time for this process; the adults need to be more present and create a reassuring, safe and soothing ambiance to wake up to, as the child will probably be waking in a fearful state.

There is evidence that children who have experienced persistent trauma in infancy have lower cortisol levels in the morning. Cortisol is a hormone that helps children overcome the effects of adrenal release caused by high levels of anxiety. It may be that your child has low morning cortisol levels when they should have higher levels to help them get up and get going. This adrenal/cortisol imbalance can only be addressed by calming, soothing and sensitive caring that will lower anxiety levels and therefore the levels of adrenaline. It would also be important to think about your child's blood sugar levels throughout the day and whether warm milk or a smoothie on waking, prior to attempting to get them ready for the day, would help. This boost of blood sugar may help to motivate the child and overcome their deficiency in cortisol. A child with low blood sugar levels will feel lethargic and may describe themselves as feeling "ill" and weak.

Should self-soothing behaviour be encouraged?

Lots of children and adults use self-soothing behaviour to help them settle to sleep. Children who have been traumatised may well have several self-soothing strategies that they have come to reply upon. If these strategies are not causing other problems, then it should not be necessary to think about discouraging them.

If children have a favourite teddy or blanket, or anything else to help them sleep, it would be advisable to ensure that you have a back-up in the wings, so that if the special one is lost, or needs eventually to be washed, you have as exact as possible a substitute ready to step in. But it may not smell right to the child, so perhaps the substitute needs to be introduced into the bed to become imbued with the right smell at an earlier stage. It is helpful for the child to be a party to this back-up role of teddy or blanket or whatever, so that the novelty will not invalidate the purpose when it is needed.

If the self-soothing aid is a teething ring or dummy, this does impact on the development of the mouth and teeth, and should be discouraged over time, but early on in a placement would certainly not be the right time to attempt to remove it.

All of these aids to self-soothing can be linked to sensory

integration strategies that we all need and use to help regulate our sensory system. Understanding your child's sensory profile will help you work out how to support them. Of course, you also need to take into account that your sensory profile may be very different from theirs, and what they need to self-soothe may not be the same as what you imagine would help them.

Some children who have been neglected and abused will masturbate to self-soothe, and this can worry parents and carers. It does not necessarily mean that they have been sexually abused, and could be the only way they have found to soothe themselves when left alone at night in discomfort. It is important that parents do not convey the message that this is bad or "dirty", but rather explore alternative strategies with the child. Children in Romanian orphanages (Rutter *et al*, 1998) were found to use self-soothing masturbation, for as they had no physical contact from an adult and were left alone in their cots, they had to find ways to touch themselves. This has also been found to be the case for other children who have suffered profound neglect. Touch releases feel-good hormones like oxytocin. These hormones are a critical and important factor in the attachment/bonding relationship, which starts with mothers and babies through breast-feeding and continues throughout childhood to adult coupling. The aim here would be to think about how to help your child form an attachment relationship to you, so that they move away from self-reliance to using their parent/carer to soothe and touch them in a non-sexualised way.

Finally, all behaviour is a communication, and we would urge no parent or carer to jump to conclusions about the degree of their child's neglectful experiences or the likelihood of sexual abuse, but to "log" the behaviour as something that might be giving important information about that child's early experiences. It could trigger a dialogue with the child in a developmental stage-appropriate way about the fact that they were scared at night, and that is how they learned to cope with their fears, but you are there for them now, and they do not have to cope on their own.

Can therapy help?

Children who have had early traumatic experiences may well need therapeutic support, and every therapy should take into account all aspects of a child's development, including their sleep pattern. What we know is that if a child does not sleep, they are not going to be able to function as well as they should, and their ability to cope with stress and to problem solve will be reduced. We also know that their physical health, in the longer term, and their ability to fight infection will be impacted. This is why a holistic approach is always advisable.

You can improve the sleep routine of your child in the ways that we have suggested, for going to sleep is a learned behaviour. However, it may need the support of a therapist to enable a traumatised child to calm, relax and sleep. The developmentally traumatised child needs to go back through the stages they missed, to learn how to sleep well. The traumatised child is stuck in the past. Developmental re-parenting, together with therapeutic intervention, should be designed to enable them to live in the present and to think about the future.

From a neuro-physiological psychotherapy perspective, sleep difficulties originate from dysfunctional regulation and poor attachment relationships caused by abuse, neglect, and poor parenting as well as multiple losses and transitions. Neuro-physiological psychotherapy offers an evidence-based inter-disciplinary holistic approach to helping traumatised children and their families.

Dyadic therapeutic approaches that address these issues include:

- Neuro-physiological psychotherapy:
  www.familyfutures.co.uk

- Theraplay:
  www.wp.theraplay.org

- Dyadic Developmental Psychotherapy:
  www.ddpnetwork.org

- Sensory Integration Therapy:
  www.sensoryintegration.org.uk

What about sleep consultants?

Sleep consultants tend to be individuals with a range of professional backgrounds offering a sleep consultancy service on a freelance paying basis, that can involve an overnight session in the family home to provide support. Professionals' backgrounds vary, from nursing and midwifery to being a parent of children who have had sleep issues. Sleep consultants are not registered or regulated, so there is no overarching quality assurance. However, there seems to be some evidence from consumer feedback that parents have found their services helpful. Our caveat is that their clientele tend to be birth families with infants and young children who are struggling with sleep patterns. In our experience, they do not have an attachment and trauma focus; their approach is primarily behavourial, and follows the controlled crying model, which deals with the sleep issue without treating the underlying trauma. Sleep consultants may or may not be funded by the local authority or Adoption Support Fund, as they are not a recognised intervention.

SECTION I

Conclusion

Here are some do's and don'ts that sum up the advice provided in earlier chapters.

Don't

- Don't blame yourself for any sleep difficulties that emerge post-placement; they will have their origins in the child's past.

- Don't get into a negative spiral of sleep deprivation and shame and blame with your partner (if you have one) and child.

- Don't think that there are quick or easy short-term solutions to sleep problems, but do remember that there are solutions and change is possible.

Do

- Do seek help and don't struggle on your own – try your social worker and GP in the first instance.

- Do take into account your own need for sleep and that none of us can do well when we are exhausted.

- Do share the sleep routine with your partner (if you have one).

- Do seek help from a friend or family member if you are a single parent.

- Do regard your child's sleep difficulties as symptomatic of living in a fearful state because of their past – this will help you, as a parent/carer, to have empathy.

- Do keep a sleep diary and look at the interrelationship between sleep, food, toileting, attachment, life events and anniversaries.

- Do think "sensory" and study your child's sensory profile, and see yourself as a sensory detective and regulator.

- Do consider melatonin, on medical advice, if other interventions need enhancing.

A final thought

Although this book is primarily about sleep and sleeping difficulties of children who are fostered or adopted, what is at the core of our approach is that helping children sleep is also primarily about helping them recover from significant harm, neglect, abuse, multiple losses and transitions, and enabling them to form meaningful and loving attachment relationships. We hope that parents and carers will see that helping their children to have healthy sleep patterns is intimately tied up with helping their children to be healthy and to have healthy relationships with them and others. Sleep is vital for our healthy development and for our capacity to cope with everyday life and to manage the usual life stressors. The importance of sleep is not to be underestimated. In order for our children to become healthy adults with functioning immune systems, we need to take sleep very seriously as a key focus for good parenting. If you sleep well, you live well.

PARENTING CHILDREN AFFECTED BY SLEEP ISSUES

A cry for help and a response: Luke's story

Mary Wood

What came before/our back story

I always wanted to have lots of children. When I was 16, I told my school class that I wanted to 'get a Master's degree and have six children', and they all laughed. I'm still not sure which part sounded funnier to them! Getting a Master's degree was something that I knew how to do: go to university, read and study and graduate. Finding a partner and having children, however, was something that eluded me for many years. I met my husband, Michael, when I was 35, but I was sure that I would find it hard to have children since many of my friends had struggled to get pregnant. Surprisingly, I was pregnant quickly and had our birth son, Oliver, in 2012. I felt that I could put a tick in the "have children" box and have no more anxiety about it. But it didn't turn out that way. My husband and I loved being parents and waited until our son was two before trying for another child. I got pregnant within a few months. We were overjoyed but, sadly, I had a miscarriage at 11 weeks. I was left shocked and deeply sad. It took more than a year for me to become pregnant again. This time I made it to nine weeks before having a miscarriage. During this time, I distanced myself from many friends who, by then, were having their second and third children. It was just too painful to see them. I felt on the outside of their happiness. Two more years went by without getting pregnant, so we decided to try IVF. I got pregnant on the first round but then had a third miscarriage, at 11 weeks. We had more rounds of IVF but began to consider adopting a child instead of continuing the fertility treatment.

We talked to Oliver about the possibility of adoption and he was excited about it. He had been asking us for a brother or sister. We knew, though, that at age five he couldn't understand how long the process we were embarking upon would take, so we talked about a brother or sister arriving when he was older. His positive attitude and excitement helped us to move forward. Whenever he asked how much longer it would be until a brother or sister arrived, we would say that we didn't know but that we hoped it would be soon. We used this time to help him understand the concept of birth and adopted children by writing a life story book for him. We used the template from our adoption training day and it proved such an important book for him. He still reads it weekly, enjoys seeing photos of his extended family and learning about his development as a young child. We knew that our adopted child would come with a life story book, so we wanted Oliver to have something similar.

Our family and adoption

My mother was adopted at birth, and my husband was adopted by his stepdad when his mother remarried, so adoption is something with which we feel comfortable. Michael and I had talked about adoption even before we were married, but always thought we would do it after having two or three birth children.

We spent a lot of time talking about the type of child that would fit in best with our lifestyle and with our son. We narrowed it down to a boy or girl of under 18 months, who possibly had a medical condition but was developing normally. Our birth son has a medical condition, but is doing so well that we felt able to cope with medical uncertainty, but not with known developmental issues.

Finding Luke

Our assessment took more than a year. Three months after we were approved, and two days after Christmas, I got an alert about a six-month-old boy with a medical condition who lived on the other side of the country. His bubbly personality and cheeky smile leapt out of the photos. His name, Luke, is also special for us as it's a name that we've always liked. Luke's birth mother used drugs extensively throughout the pregnancy, so Luke was born with drug withdrawal symptoms and spent two weeks in intensive care before being discharged to foster care. We felt comfortable with this, having read quite a lot about parental substance misuse. We had to come to terms with some uncertainty about Luke's future development.

We were hopeful that he might be placed with us by March, but the process ended up taking nearly six months.

We didn't tell Oliver about Luke until two weeks before introductions. Luke's medical condition was raised at every meeting, and we were given a long list of possible complications in the future. This was important, of course, and could be why it had been hard for the local authority to find a home for this cute little boy.

Introductions

Luke's foster carers were really nice and easy to talk to, but we were not warned that they didn't have a day or night routine for him. He slept when he wanted to and woke many times each night. He was never put back in his cot without being fully asleep. The foster carer gave him formula each time he woke, so he was getting far more formula than an 11-month-old should, and therefore wasn't very interested in other food.

During introductions, Michael and I began to feel worried about Luke's sleep pattern at night. We also found that his day-time naps were not regular. We tried to follow what the foster carer told us to do: give him formula, rock him back to sleep and lay him down gently, but it just did not work that easily for us. He was a big baby and it was hard for me to hold him in the way that the foster carer did. She is physically much bigger than me, and Luke didn't seem able to settle on my shoulder in the same way. I tried to be hopeful that in our house he would settle into a routine and things would be fine. But we knew that there would be a lot for us to do.

After 11 days, when we had worked up to caring for Luke all day in his foster placement, we went home. The foster carers brought Luke down on the train the next day and stayed in a local hotel for two days while he got used to our home.

It was a tearful goodbye when Luke's foster carers left. I'm really grateful to them for the positive and loving part they played in his life, but it would've helped us so much if Luke had been on a routine for eating and sleeping.

Luke in his new home

Once Luke was with us, we devised a tentative day and night-time routine. We were trying to stick with what he was used to during the night by giving him formula when he woke up and rocking him back to sleep. My husband and I took it in turns to get up, one night on and one night off, so that we could get a full night's sleep on alternate nights. Trying to stick with the foster carer's plan partially worked for my husband, who is similar in height to the foster carer so could hold him in the same way, but for me it didn't work at all. Luke would scream and turn away from me when I picked him up. He was waking each hour some nights and would try to push me away and take more than an hour to fall asleep every time. Even when he did fall asleep, he would wake again as soon as I put him down. I sometimes went through the feeding, rocking, holding and laying down cycle four times in a row before telling Michael that I couldn't carry on. I was shocked by how difficult this stage was, even though friends had told me that I might feel rejected. Until it happened, I had no idea how upsetting it would be. I started crying regularly, both from exhaustion but also because I was not able to comfort Luke. My husband had adoption leave from his work so we were both around to care for Luke and Oliver, but it was not easy. Oliver also started waking up in the night when Luke screamed for hours and wouldn't settle. We moved Oliver to a bedroom in the loft, further away from Luke, and this helped. We put a noisy fan in Oliver's room to drown out the noise and that seemed to help too. I don't know what we would have done if we hadn't had the loft room.

I started to feel anxious in the early evening, thinking about the coming night. How many hours would he be awake, screaming and refusing to be soothed by me? What would I do? There were days of wondering why I thought we should adopt, or maybe, that we had the wrong child. The fact that we were "seasoned" parents and thought that we should know what to do did not help us. I wondered if I had post-adoption depression, since a friend had mentioned this as a possibility. I know now that I was just so tired.

Desperately seeking help

I went online daily and searched for help. My searches for "adopted child with sleep problem" didn't produce very much that was useful. Some sites urged us not to change his routine from foster care, and not to try to force him to sleep if he didn't want to. Some information made me feel much worse for even wanting to deal with the sleeping problem. Our social worker asked us not to change anything since Luke had only been with us a month. I felt truly alone, with no advice on what to do, and feeling that I had to follow what the foster carer had done, even though she didn't have a strategy for helping him to sleep in the night. It was a dark time of walking around in a haze and seeing friends who would congratulate us and tell us how cute Luke was. Inside, I would be thinking that he wasn't cute at all, but was a bad baby who had ruined our sleep. Michael could see how unsettled Luke was with me at night, and because he worried about my state of mind, he began to deal with all the night-time wake-ups. It was such a loving and selfless thing to do, and it helped to reduce the growing tension between us. It was very hard to accept though, and to see Michael so tired each day.

Then our social worker suggested that Luke might be wanting more comfort at night, that we should put a mattress on the floor in his room to sleep with him. I tried this, and he crawled around the room for six hours! I kept bringing him back to the mattress calmly, but he would crawl away again and laugh. It was the worst night I had with him. By the morning, I had slept about one hour and had no hope of Luke ever sleeping through the night. We had no plan for what to do, and Michael and I started arguing about everything: why we had adopted, how Oliver was adjusting, whether we would ever change Luke's sleep pattern. It put such a huge strain on our relationship that my parents commented on how bad things seemed to be.

My daily Googling had led me to something helpful, though. I had found that there were sleep consultants who had special training in getting babies to sleep and that they could come and help us. I mentioned it to our social worker and she said that we should not bring anyone else into the house so early on. Then, while dropping Oliver off at school, a friend mentioned that a sleep consultant had helped her many years ago. This

65

friend is a paediatrician and I trust her judgement. I went home and looked up every sleep consultant I could find. I searched for one with adoption experience or attachment training. I found a sleep consultant based near where we live, and met with her two days later. She had many years of experience and offered to come to our house to help us. It was the first time that I felt supported in seeking a solution to Luke's sleep problems. Unfortunately, this sleep consultant didn't follow through; I sent many texts asking for her to visit but she didn't reply. It was another setback. I kept looking online for other sleep consultants.

I eventually found a sleep consultant, called Susan, who had experience of working with adopted children, and phoned her. I cried on the phone whilst explaining about Luke's sleep, and how he wasn't comforted by us, and was awake for many hours each night. She was calm and reassuring and said that she could come to our house for a whole night and coach us in what to do. She would charge £500 for the night followed by a month of phone consultations. She could then visit again in the future if we needed her.

A sleep consultant: but who will pay?

Luke had a Looked After Child (LAC) review that week, and I brought up the idea of a sleep consultant again. Luke's social worker said that we were both looking very tired and that she was worried about how we could go on living like this. She had phoned me the previous week on a bad day and I had sobbed on the phone about my tiredness. In the meeting, I felt that there was some acceptance of how bad things had got.

I vowed to book the sleep consultant regardless of whether children's services would pay. I phoned Susan and booked her to come the next week. I then wrote a letter to Luke's social worker, pleading with her to pay the £500 because we had been unaware of how Luke's lack of sleep routine would impact on the placement. I was told that the local authority didn't have money for this kind of intervention. I wrote again and, this time, it was agreed. There was a light at the end of the tunnel of sleepless nights.

Waiting for the sleep consultant's visit

The sleep consultant, Susan, asked me to keep a sleep diary for three days and to write down what Luke did each day, when he slept and what he ate. This helped me to see that we had, in fact, managed to keep to a simple routine already. She encouraged us to stop the formula and not to pick him up at night. Michael didn't feel able to do this, so I agreed to take it on since he had had so many sleepless nights already. Five nights before Susan was due to come, I put Luke to bed at 7pm without him being fully asleep, and put my hand on his back in the cot, as she had told me to do. He screamed and pushed me away for an hour and 45 minutes. It was very difficult to endure but I believed that it needed to be done. He eventually went to sleep and slept for four hours, more than he had ever done before. I went in again when he woke up crying and put my hand on his back, but didn't pick him up or give him formula. He cried for almost an hour but then he slept. It took less time each night for him to get back to sleep, but he was still very distressed. By the time the sleep consultant came, he was falling asleep after 45 minutes of crying with my hand on his back.

SECTION II

The night with the sleep consultant

I was anxious about how the night would go when Susan came, but I shouldn't have been. She was a great listener and outlined five different methods for helping babies to sleep. She explained that some of these methods were not right for Luke since they involved leaving a baby alone to cry. Luke was having to deal with moving to a new family and he needed the reassurance that we were there for him. She gave us two options to help him: 'Go in every five minutes when he cries and say 'shhhhh' and put a hand on his back, or sit by his cot with a hand on his back and then sit further away each night until you're out of the room'. We went with the "five minutes" method. Susan then described how we should put Luke to bed, and we did it. She said that we should do the same things, in the same order, each night: bath, brush teeth, give formula, read a story and say good night to the room. Then put him down fully awake, say 'I love you Luke, good night', and calmly leave the room. If he cries for a full five minutes, go in and say 'shhhhh' and put a hand on his back. Then say good night and leave. If he goes on crying, go in every five minutes to reassure him until he is quiet for 30 seconds. If he's quiet for 30 seconds, reset the five-minute timer and go in only if he continues to cry. The first night, he took 45 minutes to fall asleep and then slept until 5am! We could not believe it. This was the first time that he had ever slept that long. Then we reassured him twice and he slept again until 6:30am. We both had so much hope and energy to face life and to be good parents to Luke.

Setting up a routine for Luke

Susan then talked us through how to set up a day-time

routine. She asked when Oliver needed to be dropped at, and collected from, school, so that we could work Luke's nap times around it. That was really helpful, as it became clear that he needed a shorter morning nap and a longer afternoon nap. We would get him up every morning, whether he was asleep or awake, at 6:30am. Then he would have a short morning nap from 9:45am–10:15am; and again, after lunch, he would sleep from about 12:30pm–2:15pm when I would take him to collect Oliver from school. Susan emphasised the importance of Luke being fully tired at night, and getting him up earlier from his afternoon nap would help. It felt so good to talk about a plan for the way forward. It made Michael and me feel that we were together, maybe for the first time, in our approach to Luke's sleep. Day and night, we could use exactly the same method to put him to sleep and to reassure him. Having this plan made such a positive difference to us.

After the sleep consultant

After the first night with Susan, we instituted the day and night routine and Luke settled into our family in a way that he hadn't up until that point. It gave Michael and me far more sleep at night and, though not yet perfect, it helped Luke to teach himself to fall asleep without being fed or held, and to settle again if he woke up. Luke had had dark circles under his eyes when he came to us, and we just thought that he'd always have them. But the circles started to go away as he became more rested and it was great to see him increasingly able to focus on playing and learning to walk. Without the tiredness, he was beginning to physically develop and gain more confidence. I was also feeling much more attached to him and confident in my parenting skills. We

69

were lucky to get just the type of help that we needed.

Ongoing help from Susan

For the next month, I emailed Susan every day, outlining how Luke had slept, and she offered help whenever he woke early or cried a lot at night. She assured us that we were doing the right thing and continued to suggest tweaks in the timings of the daytime naps. It made such a difference to feel that we were not on our own. She was there for us and would respond quickly if we needed help. Luke started to sleep for longer and longer stretches at night and didn't cry when we put him down for his day-time naps.

The next six months: how did it go?

For the next six months, it seemed like all of our shoulders slowly started to relax – as though we had been constantly tense and raising our shoulders against the tiredness and apprehension of the early days. I noticed this especially with Oliver. He hadn't lost a lot of sleep but he had witnessed our tiredness and frustration. We had been cross and impatient with him on many occasions. He now started to play with Luke more often and hugged him. It made us all calm down. One day, I found a handwritten note on my pillow from Oliver. I started to cry as I read, 'Mum and Dad, I know that you've found it hard with all of the crying. Here's a toy as a present for all of your hard work. Love, Oliver'. It's the most insightful and loving thing he's ever done and will stay with me always. I had such terrible guilt about not being able to help him more in the transition to becoming an older sibling as well as shouting so much and not being as loving to him as I had been before Luke arrived. This letter made us feel like we could go on as a family of four and enjoy each other.

The future: is it rosy?

I wish that I could say that Luke's sleep pattern has stayed consistently good. Some weeks he still wakes four or five times a night and screams the house down. These times are difficult for us and we drag ourselves through tiring days. Often, the sleep disturbance is caused by him having a cold or teething. What is really different now is not that Luke never cries, but that we know what to do. We continue with the five-minute reassurance system, whether by day or night, and it helps us to remain calm and shows Luke that we are confident and are always there for him. He will not be left to cry for hours without reassurance; we will always come in every five minutes.

Luke is now 20 months old and is doing very well. Sleeping for longer stretches has meant that he can relax and continue to attach to us. He has learned to walk and run, as well as say simple words like "da da" and "ma ma". His medical condition has meant that we've taken him to hospital appointments and sought help from specialists. The prognosis at this point seems very good for a bright and full life. He has begun to show his independence by throwing toys, sometimes at us and Oliver, and not wanting to get into the pram. I take him to a special playgroup for adopted children and often seek out the social workers there to talk about his behaviour and what is normal. A few weeks ago, I met someone else with a birth child who has now adopted, and it meant so much to me that she shares some of our early experiences. She also faces sleeping difficulties and

I was able to tell our story and offer some hope.

It's such a big relief to have Luke with us and to know that he will be with us forever. His celebration hearing was a few weeks ago. It was a very short, and yet meaningful moment to celebrate all that has happened. Luke smiled for the photos with the judge and Oliver asked the judge all about his job. He was most excited to tell his friends at school about meeting a "real" judge.

I hope that our story can offer encouragement to others. It's likely that many adopters are able to slowly adjust the sleeping patterns of their new child without the need for a sleep consultant. For us, it just didn't work out that way, and I'm so glad that there are people who have specialist training in sleep. It is probably what kept us together as a family!

Comment by authors

What is clear from this case study is the complexity even of infant placements, and the need to attend to key issues around sleep, food, toileting and attachment that have not been resolved in foster care. This case highlights that usual behavioural strategies and social work advice are insufficient when placing a baby with an inherited medical condition or drug withdrawal symptoms. The problems for this little boy did not begin at birth but in utero, where the mother's mental stress hormones and use of drugs would have crossed the placenta and impacted on the foetus. One book aptly describes the phenomenon as being "bruised before birth" (McNamara et al, 1995).

It is shocking to read the degree of distress that the

family was in and the lack of wrap-around support, so that they had to seek a private sleep consultant. This sleep consultant then successfully incorporated the child's trauma history into the strategy of sleep management and "controlled crying". The systematic and structured approach is sensible and clearly effective for Luke and helps the whole family to settle. It also importantly highlights how, if no one in the family is sleeping, it affects all family members and, vitally, also has an impact on burgeoning attachment relationships. Clearly Luke and sleep are still at times an issue, but the family has largely found a positive way forward, which is really hopeful. It also highlights how important getting expert help may be to avoid disruption of a placement.

SECTION II

A good night's sleep: Jessie's story

Jayne Lilley

Introduction

A good night's sleep was something that we took for granted at the time we adopted Jessie in 2014, when she was just one year old. Our family then consisted of my husband, Dan, me, and our five-year-old birth son, Charlie. We had all long forgotten those early years and the broken sleep, but it came back to us with a vengeance on Jessie's first night in our home. Unsurprisingly, we were awoken hourly as she found it difficult to settle. We did expect this in the first weeks, so I slept on a mattress on the floor next to her cot, to comfort her and make her feel she wasn't alone.

During the "introduction" stages, when we began to look after Jessie in her foster home in the lead-up to bringing her home, I'd had some wonderful and memorable moments with Jessie. She'd never fallen asleep while being held by anyone before, but did so with me on our second day of meeting. This, I think, led to a feeling of over-confidence and let me believe that the transition would be plain sailing. Of course, it was easy for Jessie to be happy and relaxed in the only home, and with the only carers, she'd ever known, in the room with us. At this point, I was no more than a friendly visitor and it would probably have helped to have remembered that.

We tried our best to replicate the bedroom that Jessie had slept in by keeping her new room uncluttered, with a simple cot without toys, but despite our best efforts Jessie found her new room strange to sleep in. To compound matters, Jessie had shared the room in the foster home with another baby who was the same age as her, and no doubt they would babble together and comfort each other during the night. As we didn't have a child of the same age, I slept in the room, hoping that if Jessie woke and heard another person breathing, it would be enough comfort. As inconvenient as a lack of sleep was for all of us, we couldn't forget that Jessie had been taken away from everything familiar without warning, and moved into the home of strangers. I can't pretend to be able to imagine how bewildering and frightening that must have been for her. All we could do, we thought, was to be patient and consistent in our reactions and to stick to her daily routine. She must have been immensely anxious in those first days when she woke hourly in a strange environment with strangers attempting to soothe her. We hoped routine would help to bring about familiarity and trust, and I agreed an extended 14-month adoption leave period with my employer to help Jessie to attach to her new family. However more sleep deprived and irritable we became, it seemed really important to remain calm and hide any signs of the internal panic that we were actually feeling. It was natural to feel anxious, particularly since we had felt so supported throughout introductions, and although we had support from health workers, social workers and could ask for advice from Jessie's foster carer during the day, at night we were really on our own.

It became a true exercise in patience. When Jessie was tired, she would whine relentlessly; it was a constant background noise. If her feelings of upset escalated, she would scream, and these screams would be loud and often directly into your face, and usually coupled with hitting out. We would then have to wait for her to calm down before carrying on with whatever activity we were involved in.

In adoption training, social workers talk about not reacting to challenging behaviour, and the videos and training material focus on verbal children, and offer strategies if they refuse or ignore what you ask them to do. But it should not be underestimated how non-verbal babies are able to challenge by their behaviour. Our experience was that Jessie refused to eat, refused to be toilet trained, and hit out at us. But the biggest impact on both Jessie and us was interrupted sleep and the results of sleep deprivation for five years of our lives.

Nightmares and night terrors

Before Jessie, I had no experience of severe nightmares and night terrors. Charlie had a couple of sleepwalking episodes when aged six, that coincided with SATs and were no doubt stress-related. Once SATs were over, they stopped, and he hasn't had any since. With Jessie, the issues with sleep were ongoing from the day we brought her home, and continued for five years. The peak and worst period of sleeplessness was between the ages of three and five. Jessie would wake up to four times every night.

In the early years before Jessie could speak, she was, of course, unable to tell us what was wrong when she woke, and we would simply sit with her and stroke her face until she went back to sleep. By the age of three, the nightmares intensified and became "night terrors". The first time, Dan and I were woken in the early hours of the morning by the sound of Jessie hysterically screaming. I ran into her room to find her sitting bolt upright, eyes open, petrified, and thrashing as if fighting something or someone to keep away from her. I did the most natural but worst thing possible; I attempted to console her, but Jessie hit out and continued to thrash around in her bed whilst repeatedly shouting 'no' between screams. Even though it appeared that her eyes were looking at me, she didn't see me; she was still asleep despite the outward appearance of being very much awake. The only course of action, we found out, was to sit beside her silently and make sure that she didn't hurt herself.

It used to take Jessie around 20 minutes before she came out of the frantic state, laid down and appeared to go back to normal sleep. I would sit with her and stroke her head until I was sure that she was sound asleep again.

For me, however, it was impossible to return to

sleep after witnessing these incidents; they were overwhelming, the primary feeling for me was one of helplessness mixed with panic and fear – it can only be likened to watching someone possessed, fighting against something or someone that wasn't there. The next morning, when Jessie woke after one of these "terrors", she would have no recollection of the episode. Given the intensity of the experience, I found this puzzling.

The terrors happened routinely at the same time each night, and Jessie's reaction was always the same: I'd find her sitting bolt upright in bed, repeatedly shouting 'no' and fighting off whatever she saw at the end of her bed, with eyes wide open. I spoke to health visitors and explained what was happening and they told me about night terrors, said that they were normal for some children and that she would grow out of them; they didn't seem overly concerned. Although we had an older child, we had never experienced any of these sleep disturbances, and were uncertain about whether they affected a lot of children or if they were more prevalent in adopted children. I discovered that a friend's son had suffered night terrors, and she said they had lasted for around a year and stopped as abruptly as they had started. It was comforting to chat with someone who had been through a similar experience.

On researching night terrors, I was pleased to find that I'd done the right thing by not disturbing or trying to wake Jessie, but staying with her, ready to intervene if she looked as though she was going to hurt herself. The advice given to prevent night terrors was to gently wake the child 10 minutes before the usual terror time, the aim being to break an established cycle.

We followed the suggestion, but for Jessie it simply seemed to delay the episode; it just happened later. Night after night, I sat with her, until after a year she stopped having night terrors – just as my friend had predicted!

Despite the terrors having come to an end, Jessie still didn't sleep well and had more traditional nightmares. She would wake up with the same alarmed scream but would recognise me when I came into her room, and once consoled, she would be able to tell me what had frightened her. The nightmares were repetitive and had a similar theme: they either concerned a boy who would stare and point at her, insects crawling on her or, more recently, being abandoned by family members. Whenever these nightmares occur, and Jessie has calmed down and can speak about them, we talk about events that may have upset her, and I will touch her forehead and say, 'I'm taking that bad dream away'. We'll then talk about a good memory, and once she's smiling and happy, I'll say, 'You can have that memory', and will touch her forehead, putting the memory about a day at the beach, or whatever it may be, into her head. It has become a little ritual that seems to work, and she then manages to sleep until morning.

Triggers

By getting to know Jessie over the course of time, we got to know that challenging behaviour and disrupted sleep were not purely random; there was always a trigger, an event during the day that had either upset, frightened or made Jessie feel uncomfortable, and the resulting anxiety was expressed in the form of a nightmare.

One of the triggers we knew about was any kind of change, and unfortunately, during the first two years of Jessie's life with us (aged one–three), there was a lot of upheaval, which we expected to have a short-term effect, but felt would be good for the family in the long term. We could have avoided change, but certain opportunities presented themselves and we had to weigh up whether long-term improvement would be beneficial for us all, in spite of the effect it might have on Jessie. We also wanted to help her to manage change rather than avoid it; to feel more confident about new situations rather than be anxious about them, because we felt that avoiding change altogether would be more detrimental in the long run.

The first, and the change with the biggest impact, was my return to full-time work after 14 months' adoption leave. Jessie was to start at the local private nursery that Charlie had attended, and which had given him a lovely head start both socially and academically. We were delighted to discover that five years later, most of the same nursery staff still worked there. Jessie had the usual settling-in period, and all seemed fine; she bonded well with her nursery carer, who adored Jessie. The days were long for her: from 7.30am until she was collected at 6pm. As soon as we collected her from the nursery, she started to scream and cry, and this would continue on the journey home and once we got home. We assumed at first that it was tiredness after the long day, and that she would sleep as soon as she settled down in her cot, but when we put her to bed she wouldn't lie down or settle at all. We tried the usual methods to calm her: a quiet time with lots of cuddles after dinner and before going to bed, a warm bath with lavender oil and into lovely warm pyjamas – but to no avail.

It was a strange phenomenon; we could see that Jessie was tired and she would almost drift off to sleep, but then would stop herself and wake herself up. With the benefit of hindsight, I can say that Jessie was overstimulated at nursery, and at the same time, the change to seeing me less than before must have made her too anxious to let herself sleep. She was too young at this point to articulate her feelings and I can only guess what they were by her behaviour and sleeping difficulties.

We decided that as I was back at work, we would book a holiday in Spain during the children's summer holidays. We thought that it would be nice to have something for us all to look forward to, and get some sunshine, so we booked 12 months in advance, giving us plenty of time to prepare Jessie for the change of environment. We chose Spain, as the flight time was manageable for her and she was excited at the prospect of flying, especially after we took her to the local airport to watch the planes take off and land. What we didn't consider was that 12 months is a long time and a lot can happen in that time, and happen it did!

The house that we had lived in for the past eight years was in the built-up suburb of a city, and once Jessie joined the family the house suddenly became very small with four people living in it. Although we weren't looking to move, we always knew that this house was a stop-gap until we found the home that we wanted to live in long term.

Whilst driving to a forest close by, we drove past a house that was for sale in a village that I'd always liked, around 20 minutes' drive away from where we

SECTION II

lived. It was a larger detached house in a semi-rural location facing fields, and very close to the forest that we enjoyed visiting most weekends. We went to look at it, and instantly knew that it was the home for us, especially after both Jessie and Charlie picked their bedrooms and asked when we could move in. We knew that it was the right move for the family and could see the benefits almost immediately – both Charlie and Jessie love being outdoors and exploring nature, and we thought that living in a semi-rural location would have a calming influence. We just wanted to improve our quality of life, slow down and relax a little; finding the house in that location was the perfect solution.

While waiting for the sale to complete, we would show Jessie and Charlie pictures of their rooms, so that it wouldn't be such a surprise when we finally moved. We visited the local village shops, the park, and walked around the area, so that both children became familiar with the village and the look of our new house prior to the move.

However, there was a problem: the completion date for the purchase was the day when we were due to fly to Spain. We would leave our home to go on holiday for two weeks, and then return home to a new house.

The probable impact of this on Jessie and Charlie was not lost on us, but for various administrative and financial reasons, the dates were non-negotiable.

The holiday itself was dreadful; Jessie wouldn't sleep on her own, so shared with me for two weeks. Both children loved swimming, and the hotel had four children's swimming areas, but Jessie decided that she didn't like the pools, so she and I were on our own for most of the time. Dan and I hadn't slept for a full night in 12 months, and by this point our judgement and problem-solving skills were severely impaired. We both worked full time in stressful management roles after sleepless nights, and we would still try to keep up the energy levels with our children – we were both careering towards burn-out.

We flew back to the UK and drove straight to an unfamiliar house. There was too much change in a short space of time, and our attempts to prepare the children did not prepare them for the reality.

I hadn't been able to transfer Jessie's nursery school place to the local school as it was oversubscribed, and Charlie hadn't wanted to change school either, so the children had to be up, dressed, fed and ready to leave at 7am promptly. I had passed my driving test in readiness for the move. It was essential in order for me to get to work and to take the children to school now that we were living out of town.

Sleep became an immediate issue, as expected after the move, and we tried all our usual methods of stroking Jessie's face, using night lights and leaving bathroom lights on. The new house was an L-shaped cottage dating back to the 1800s, with two bedrooms next to each other at one side of the L, and the master bedroom at the other side. We decided that Charlie would sleep in the master bedroom, and Dan and I would take the room next to Jessie. We would be able to comfort her more easily during the night and Charlie would be undisturbed.

Jessie did suffer the expected nightmares, and would wake several times during the night and scream loudly. We were so exhausted by this point that she either ended up in our bed or one of us went to sleep in hers. The effect of sleep deprivation on Dan and I was profound. I would drive the children to nursery and school, which now took 30 minutes. Jessie would be tired and fractious and often wouldn't want to get into the car seat; she would shout at the top of her voice whilst I was driving. I'd have to pull over and wait until she was calm before driving on. Dan and I often felt as though we were in constant battle mode and it was affecting both our physical and mental health. We all felt exhausted from lack of sleep; Dan and I were constantly trying to find ways to deal with the sleep issues, and we were focusing all our efforts on Jessie and feared that Charlie would feel pushed out. We didn't feel as though we could ever use a babysitter or allow Jessie to stay with family members until the sleeping difficulties had been resolved – there was no respite from the situation that we were in!

After much deliberation and discussion, we decide that the best course of action was for me to drastically reduce my working hours. I was out of the house for 12 hours each day in a highly stressful environment. We needed to make a profound change to help Jessie settle down in the new house. We hoped that our decision would help her sleep pattern to improve.

Yet another change was looming large: Jessie was due to start at the local school that September, and I wanted to be around to help her manage this huge, approaching transition. Once my working hours reduced, there was an almost immediate improvement: I was more relaxed and could fully focus on the children and their needs; I could catch up with sleep in the day so that I could cope with the broken nights, and Dan could be undisturbed and fresh for work next day – it was a big decision, a change with huge financial implications, but it was necessary in order to bring harmony and routine into our home.

School

The school that Jessie was to attend had a lovely head of reception who visited her in her pre-school setting to get to know her, and have a little chat about school and how she felt about it. I don't think that Jessie really understood that she would be leaving her nursery, friends and care workers, but we tried our best to manage the change. I'd had a couple of long telephone conversations with the head of reception and had raised concerns about the impact of the change and the fact that she might regress. I explained that Jessie was adopted – they weren't aware of it, which I found surprising. I had naturally assumed that the school would have this information, especially since we had submitted a claim for Pupil Premium Plus, an annual grant awarded to schools to assist looked after and adopted children.

Before Jessie was due to start school, we met the reception teachers and discovered that there were only three children in the reception year who hadn't attended the pre-school class, so it might be that the children would all have established friendships from the two years at pre-school and nursery.

We tried to prepare Jessie for the change to come by visiting the local park where children went to play after school. We would walk around the village and past the school and encourage her to talk about any worries.

A new issue came to light that had to be resolved before she started in the new school. We were having some problems with Jessie having tummy pain caused by constipation, largely because she would not use the toilet at her old school. 'It could explain some of the present sleeping difficulties', we thought; 'stomach-ache could be waking her up during the night alongside the anxiety due to change'.

In order to relive the symptoms, I gave her lots of water to drink, hid fruit and vegetables in her meals, added vitamins to aid digestion plus tummy massage and warm baths. The combination worked and we finally all got a good night's sleep.

We had managed to resolve most of the sleeping difficulties just before the beginning of term in the new school, but we were acutely aware how any changes in routine could cause a regression. The head of year suggested that we use a communication book, so that we could alert the school of any notable changes at home, and the school staff would do the same. Despite our worries, all was well for the first term and we were delighted with the way Jessie managed; she made friends quickly and was coping with the new routine. She slept well and only woke if the covers fell off or if she needed the toilet. We started to feel like life might be returning to some normality; Jessie was thriving, she and a little girl called Bella, who had started in her class a bit later, got on well.

At the beginning of the second term, I received repeated

phone calls from one of the teachers about Jessie's behaviour. She would phone me at work with minor complaints, such as Jessie sticking her tongue out, which seemed rather petty; soon I was being called in regularly to attend at the end of the school day to see this particular teacher who would relay all of Jessie's minor misdemeanours with Jessie in the room; I found this wholly inappropriate. Jessie was only just four years old. Of course, this kickstarted sleepless nights again and brought on nightmares about school.

Jessie would wake up tired and anxious in the morning; on opening her eyes, the first thing she would ask was: 'Is it school today?' When we told her that it was, she would cry and refuse to go. We could coax her to get dressed by reassuring and reasoning, and get her to the school gate happily enough, but in the playground her demeanour would change; she became quiet, and clung on to my legs. At the door where we led the children into the classroom, she would try to run away. I would have to ask the teacher to take her from me while she was screaming 'Mummy' and holding her arms out to me. If I consoled her it made it worse; I just had to leave and call the school later to be told that she'd calmed down within minutes of me leaving. It seemed to me little wonder that Jessie didn't enjoy school if she was being openly and negatively discussed and punished for minor offences she probably did not understand. I suggested it was perhaps the school environment and the strict, and at times petty nature, of the rules that were hindering her learning. For example, at age four, she was marched to the headteacher for throwing a snowball at an older girl; apparently any throwing in the playground meant an immediate trip to the headteacher. Both Dan and I couldn't help but feel that Jessie was being singled out and almost made an example of. When the teacher told me about the snowball incident, Jessie was again in the room and I witnessed her physically crumple with shame. At this point, Dan and I decided that we needed to book an appointment to speak to the headteacher. Jessie's sleep was once more massively affected, and lack of sleep led to a lack of concentration and challenging behaviour.

Just before our meeting with the headteacher, there was an incident between Jessie and her friend Bella: Jessie kicked Bella and was punished as a result – she later told me that Bella had hit her first. It was general kids' stuff, but the school was very hot on behaviour. I spoke to Bella's mother and apologised, she accepted the apology, or so it seemed, and she was happy to let the teachers deal with it – very reasonable, or so I thought. The very next day I received a phone call from the head of year, as Bella's mother had discussed the situation and Bella was to be moved into a different class. Of course, the impact was huge; Jessie wouldn't sleep and absolutely refused to go to school, and who could blame her!

We told the headteacher about the constant phone calls and requests to come to school to see the teacher. She agreed that it was too much, and arranged another meeting with the head of year.

At this second meeting, we were told that Jessie was unable to socialise, attacked other children, and was not learning – it sounded as though they were talking about a different child. We would watch Jessie being kind to children in parks and to friends' children, helping them and including them. What was puzzling was that all of the work the school told us Jessie couldn't do, she could do at home. We would see her handwriting and hear her reading at home, and we didn't have any concerns regarding her progress. The school's methods seemed to be upsetting Jessie's learning and behaviour as well as her sleep. We seemed to be calming her down for the entire night after events at school, and this time we were all sleep deprived as a direct result of whatever was happening during the school day. We considered the possibility of changing schools, but Jessie had made other friends, and it seemed a drastic course of action to take. The book that was supposed to encourage communication between us and the school had descended into pettiness: I was being asked not to plait Jessie's hair because she would undo the plaits – not the original purpose of the book at all!

When we met with the headteacher, we had asked when the supposed challenging behaviour occurred. It was always in the afternoon after lunch. I asked if they monitored lunch times to ensure that children were eating, and it transpired that they did not.

When we met again a few weeks later, the head of year told us that Jessie hadn't been eating any lunch at all, so was no doubt hungry during the afternoon, which would account for her lack of attention and lack of patience. Once lunchtimes were monitored, and Jessie was being encouraged to eat her dinner, the school staff reported an immediate improvement in all areas. It seemed basic to me, and we were flabbergasted that it wasn't the first thing being checked. The reason that we had selected a small school for Jessie was so that this kind of issue could be picked up quickly and she could be helped accordingly.

We discussed ways that would help alleviate Jessie's anxiety in the school environment, and she was offered a mentor, someone special she could speak to if she was worried. They played games and read stories together to help her to get through the school day, and Jessie coped well when she knew the routine. It was when routines changed that the old issues resurfaced: any deviation from the normal school day made Jessie anxious, and the knock-on effect was always on sleep. Christmas was a particularly difficult time of year; the many activities during the winter term meant that Jessie wouldn't get a proper night's sleep, and neither would we. We were always pleased when we finally reached Christmas Day.

It was not until Jessie started in Year Two that she began to enjoy going to school. She was then six years old, there had been no more significant changes in her life and she began to sleep soundly almost every night. She still has the occasional nightmares even now, to do with separation and monsters, but these are infrequent, and normal reassurance will allay any fears.

The impact of Jessie's sleeping difficulties on us, as a family, has been immense and has touched every aspect of our lives. We chose not to socialise with friends because we were mentally and physically exhausted. We wouldn't leave Jessie with family members because it felt unfair both to her and to our family, when we knew how important routine was to her and how challenging her behaviour could be at bedtime and throughout the night.

Now that Jessie is almost seven years old and is fully settled in our family and home environment, we feel that we have made enormous progress. Jessie regularly has sleep-overs with her Nana and enjoys them enormously, and she sleeps soundly. Holidays, since the first terrible Spanish holiday, have been UK-based; we sit with Jessie until she is asleep, and providing she knows her way around our accommodation, she sleeps soundly.

It has been a huge learning experience to achieve peaceful nights with Jessie, but some strategies have consistently helped us and may help other families:

- For any change in routine, drip-feed the change beforehand: visit new places, watch videos, share photos, tell stories.

- Have a consistent bedtime routine – bath, warm pyjamas, story, face stroke and then lights out (landing light left on); night lights proved too bright and distracting.

- We tried to discourage Jessie coming into our bed, and instead slept in hers if she needed company or a cuddle until she fell asleep.

- We found calming activities at the weekend to act as a form of therapy to combat anxiety that affected sleep; horse riding, piano lessons, any activities that help to boost confidence can aid sleep.

- Spend as much time as possible outdoors at the weekend.

- Make sure that your child is not constipated or hungry before bedtime, so they won't wake with stomach-ache.

- Expect the worst in the first few weeks of placement. Be prepared to sleep on the floor near to your child to give comfort as soon as they wake, and to build trust.

- Be patient, consistent and try to stay calm.

Comment by the authors

Jessie's sleep difficulties once more highlight how crucial sleep is to the whole family, and also the lack of support and advice available. The adoptive parents do themselves find a way forward, but the process is painful and extended. It would have been much better if expert advice had been on offer from the beginning. It does not appear that Jessie's sleep difficulties and separation and relationship difficulties had been put into a life story narrative framework. It also seems that support was not offered to the family or school about how to work together to help Jessie. The fact that school staff missed the link between Jessie not eating lunch and her behaviour is sadly not uncommon. This case once more highlights the interrelationship between food, sleep, toileting and attachment, and demonstrates quite clearly how the sleep problem is not a problem in isolation for Jessie. A holistic approach to her early developmental trauma would have helped, but the parents were left to deal with the problem behaviourally. The parent's recommendations at the end are thoughtful and offer good advice that fits with our own thinking about parenting a developmentally traumatised young child.

Due to the age and stage of the children in both case examples, it was not initially possible for the parents to engage in meaningful dialogue with the children about their history; the support both children required was much more about developmental re-parenting with the focus on primitive brain calming, sensory strategies and attachment formation.

Neither family seems to have consulted health visitors, who have experience in supporting adopters and foster carers during the early years and who can provide useful advice and support.

References

Armstrong KL, O'Donnell H, McCallum R and Dadds M (2003) 'Childhood sleep problems: association with prenatal factors and maternal distress/depression', *Journal of Paediatrics and Child Health*, 34:3, pp 263–266

Booth PB and Jernburg AM (2009) *Theraplay* (3rd edn), San Francisco, CA: Jossey-Bass

DeRosa R, Hubbard R, Kagen R, Liautaud J, Mallah K, Olafson E and van der Kolk B (2005) 'Complex trauma in children and adolescents', *Psychiatric Annals*, 35:5, pp 390–398

Fenton K (2019) *Parenting a Child with Toileting Issues*, London: CoramBAAF

Ferber R (2013) *Solve Your Child's Sleep Problems*, London: Vermilion

Harvard Medical School (2006) *The Importance of Sleep: Six reasons not to scrimp on sleep*, Harvard, MA: Harvard Health Publishing

Hookway L (2019) *Holistic Sleep Coaching*, Amarillo, TX: Praeclarus Press

Hughes D (2013) *Parenting a Child with Emotional and Behavioural Difficulties*, London: BAAF

Kajeepeta S, Gelaye B, Jackson CL and Williams MA (2015) 'Adverse childhood experiences are associated with adult sleep disorders: a systematic review', *Sleep Medicine*, 16:3, pp 320–330

Marsh S (2017) 'Too many children being prescribed melatonin to aid sleep, experts warn', *The Guardian*, 29 May

McCullough E, Gordon Jones S, Last A, Vaughan J and Burnell J (2016) 'An evaluation of Neuro Physiological Psychotherapy: An integrative approach to working with children who have experienced early life trauma', *Journal of Clinical Child Psychology and Psychiatry*, 21:4, pp 582–602

McCullough E and Mathura A (2019) 'Control group evaluation of Neuro-Physiological Psychotherapy (NPP)', *Child Abuse & Neglect*, 97, pp 104–128

McNamara J, Bullock A and Grimes E (1995) *Bruised Before Birth: Parenting children exposed to parental substance abuse*, London: BAAF

SECTION II

Ottaway H and Selwyn J (2016) *No-One Told us it was Going to be Like This: Compassion fatigue and foster carers*, Bristol: University of Bristol

Owens J (2008) 'Classification and epidemiology of childhood sleep disorders', *Primary Care: Clinics in Office Practice*, 35:3, pp 533–546

Rutter M and the English Romanian Adoptees Study Team (1998) 'Developmental catch up, and deficit, following adoption after severe global early privation', *Journal of Child Psychology and Psychiatry*, 39:4, pp 465–476

Vaughan J, McCullough E and Burnell A (2016) 'Neuro Physiological Psychotherapy (NPP): The development and application of an integrative wrap around service and treatment programme for maltreated children placed in adoptive and foster care placements', *Journal of Clinical Child Psychology and Psychiatry*, 21:4, pp 568–581

Glossary

Co-sleeping
This essentially means sleeping in close proximity to your child. It may be in the same bed or just in the same room.

Developmental trauma
This is not a formal diagnosis, but is terminology that is now generally accepted as the best way of describing the developmental impact of trauma on a child's development.

Dyadic Developmental Psychotherapy (DDP)
A dyadic therapy, parenting approach and model for practice that uses what we know about attachment and developmental trauma to help children and families with their relationships.

Extraceptive information

Information that we all gather from the environment around us through our senses.

Introceptive information

Information that we all gather through our senses about our internal physiological state and body functions.

Melatonin

A natural hormone that is produced by the pineal gland (located in the brain). It helps control the sleep cycle. The body produces melatonin just after it gets dark, peaking in the early hours of the morning and reducing during daylight hours. Melatonin acts on receptors in the body to encourage sleep.

Mentalisation

The ability to understand the mental state of oneself or others and what underlies their motivation, so it is the ability to understand one's own and others' intentions.

Neuro-biological

A term that refers to the physiology of the brain and the body as well as the interconnection between the two.

Neuro-physiological psychotherapy (NPP)

A dyadic therapy for children who are traumatised and have attachment difficulties. It integrates a range of different disciplines and therapeutic approaches to provide an integrative wrap-around therapy. It also works with the family as a whole and their wider network.

Neuroscience

A body of knowledge that has grown rapidly in the

last 25 years, that relates to research and theorising about the brain and central nervous system and their functioning.

Neuro-sequential

A therapeutic approach that follows the development of the brain and nervous system from the primitive brain, to the mid (limbic) brain, to the higher cortical brain (cortex). This approach moves from a regulatory focus, to an attachment relationship focus, to problem-solving and reflective capacity.

Neuro-typical

A term that is now used as a way to describe individuals with typical developmental, emotional and cognitive abilities. In other words, it is not used to describe individuals who have some form of diagnosable difference.

Night terrors

Episodes of screaming, intense fear and flailing while still asleep. Also known as sleep terrors, night terrors are often paired with sleepwalking. Like sleepwalking, night terrors are considered a "parasomnia", which is an undesired occurrence during sleep.

Self-regulation

The ability of a child or adult to be able to regulate emotional feeling states themselves without the assistance of another person.

Sensory Integration Assessment

There is now a body of evidence that shows that children who have experienced poor parenting or trauma in infancy are likely to have sensory processing and developmental difficulties of some kind and varying in degrees of severity. A Paediatric Occupational Therapist (OT) Sensory Integration Assessment looks in more depth at sensory motor skills, visual perception, activities of daily living and sensory processing in the context of developmental trauma. This is a specialist sensory integration assessment, not usually provided on the NHS, and requires the skills of a specialist sensory integration trained Occupational Therapist (trained to at least SI level 4), and who is experienced with working with traumatised and adopted children.

Sensory Processing Disorder

A condition in which the brain has trouble receiving and responding to information that comes in through the senses. Formerly referred to as sensory integration dysfunction, it is not currently recognised as a distinct medical diagnosis.

Sleep apnoea

A serious sleep disorder that occurs when a person's breathing is interrupted during sleep. People with untreated sleep apnoea stop breathing repeatedly during their sleep, sometimes hundreds of times. This means that the brain and the rest of the body may not get enough oxygen.

Theraplay

A dyadic (looking at the interaction between two things) therapy that works with parent and child together to address behavioural, emotional and developmental issues to improve the parent–child relationship through play and healthy interaction.

Useful organisations

Family Futures

Voluntary adoption agency and independent fostering provider as well as an assessment and treatment service for traumatised children.

3 & 4 Floral Place
7–9 Southampton Grove
London N1 2P
Tel: 020 7354 4161
www.family futures.co.uk

Chrysalis Associates

A therapeutic team of professionals drawn from the fields of social work, clinical and educational psychology, who specialise in the assessment and treatment of developmental trauma and attachment difficulties.

48 Wostenholme Road
Nether Edge

Sheffield S7 1LL
Tel: 0144 2509 455
www.chrysalisassociates.org/

PAC – UK (part of Family Action)

A post-adoption support agency that offers a range of support and counselling to adopted children, families, and adopted adults.
34 Wharf Road
London N1 7GR
Tel: 020 7284 0555
Advice line: 0113 230 210
www.pac-uk.org/

Anna Freud Centre

An organisation that provides services to families and children with emotional, behavioural and developmental difficulties.
12 Maresfield Gardens
London NW3 SSU
Tel: 020 7794 2313
www.annafreud.org

Children's Sleep Charity

An organisation that supports children with sleep issues, offering a behavioural approach, in partnership with families.
Tel: 01302 752 416
www.thechildrenssleepcharity.org.uk/

PARENTING MATTERS

This unique series provides expert knowledge about a range of children's health conditions, coupled with facts, figures and guidance presented in a straightforward and accessible style. Adopters and foster carers also describe what it is like to parent an affected child, "telling it like it is", sharing their parenting experiences and offering useful advice.

To find out more visit **www.corambaaf.org.uk/bookshop**